SINGER

SEWING REFERENCE LIBRARY®

101 Sewing Secrets

Cy DeCosse Incorporated
Minnetonka, Minnesota

SINGER

SEWING REFERENCE LIBRARY®

101 Sewing Secrets

Contents

How to Use This Book 7

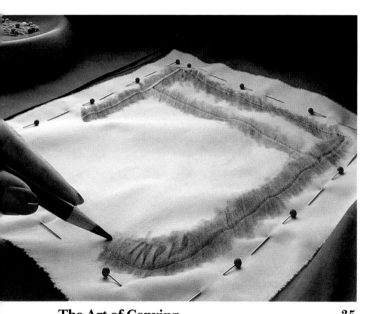

Copyright © 1989
Cy DeCosse Incorporated
5900 Green Oak Drive
Minnetonka, Minnesota 55343
1-800-328-3895
All rights reserved.
Printed in U.S.A.

Also available from the publisher: *Sewing Essentials, Sewing for the Home, Clothing Care & Repair, Sewing for Style, Sewing Specialty Fabrics, Sewing Activewear, The Perfect Fit, Timesaving Sewing, More Sewing for the Home, Sewing Update, Tailoring, Sewing for Children, Sewing with an Overlock, Sewing Pants That*

Fit, Quilting by Machine, Decorative Machine Stitching, Creative Sewing Ideas, Sewing Lingerie, Sewing Projects for the Home

Library of Congress
Cataloging-in-Publication Data

101 sewing secrets.
    p. cm. — (Singer sewing reference library)
Includes index.
ISBN 0-86573-249-3
ISBN 0-86573-250-7 (pbk.)
    1. Sewing. I. Title: one hundred one sewing secrets.
II. Series.
TT705.A12   1989
646.2'044—dc20   89-1416
                                    CIP

Distributed by: Contemporary Books, Inc.
    Chicago, Illinois

CY DE COSSE INCORPORATED
Chairman: Cy DeCosse
President: James B. Maus
Executive Vice President: William B. Jones

101 SEWING SECRETS
Created by: The Editors of Cy DeCosse
    Incorporated, in cooperation with the
    Sewing Education Department, Singer
    Sewing Company. Singer is a trademark
    of The Singer Company and is used
    under license.

Executive Editor: Zoe Graul
Technical Director: Rita C. Opseth

Project Managers: Melissa Erickson,
Ann Schlachter
Senior Art Director: Lisa Rosenthal
Assistant Art Director: Antonio Magni
Writers: Karen Drellich, Sue Green
Editors: Janice Cauley, Bernice Maehren
Contributing Editor: Mary Gannon
Sample Supervisors: Wendy Fedie,
Joanne Wawra
Sewing Staff: Phyllis Galbraith, Bridget
Haugh, Joan Coop, Sara Holmen, Julie
Muschamp, Linda Newbauer, Loy O'Boyle,
Carol Olson, Lori Ritter, Valerie Ruthardt,
Nancy Sundeen, Barb Vik, John Willcox
Fabric Editor: Marie Castle
Technical Photo Director: Bridget Haugh

Photo Studio Manager: Cathleen Shannon
Photographers: Bobbette Destiche, Rex
Irmen, Tony Kubat, John Lauenstein, Bill
Lindner, Mark Macemon, Mette Nielsen
Contributing Photographer: Doug Deutscher
Production Manager: Jim Bindas
Assistant Production Managers: Julie Churchill,
Amelia Merz
Production Staff: Russ Beaver, Holly Clements,
Sheila DiPaola, Joe Fahey, Kevin D. Frakes,
Yelena Konrardy, Scott Lamoureux, Jody
Phillips, Linda Schloegel, Greg Wallace,
Nik Wogstad
Consultants: Helen Adelsman, Roberta Carr,
Deborah Gangnon, Pam Hastings,

Gail Grigg Hazen, Janet Klaer, JoAnn
Krause, Carol Olson, Kathy Sandmann,
Nancy Sundeen, Marcy Tilton, Tammy
Young
Contributing Manufacturers: B. Blumenthal
& Co., Inc.; Burda Patterns; C. M. Offray
& Son, Inc.; Chandlers Shoes; JHB
International, Inc.; Kwik-Sew Pattern
Company; The McCall Pattern Company;
Simplicity Pattern Company, Inc; Singer
Sewing Company; Vogue/Butterick
Patterns; YKK Home Sewing Division
Color Separations: Scantrans
Printing: Ringier America, Inc. (1191)

POLYESTER
50" WIDE
2 YARDS
MACHINE W
6 5

How to Use This Book

Home sewers are always looking for methods that are easier, more efficient, or give a better-quality finish. The secrets included in this book will help you enjoy sewing more than ever.

Sewing Room Secrets

In the first section of the book, discover new ways to organize and prepare your fabric stash. Also find out how to determine the fiber content of fabrics, using the "burn test."

This section offers detailed information on the variety of pins, needles, and threads on the market and what they are used for. Selecting just the right one for the job can make each sewing project easier.

Learn how to make your own seam roll from a magazine or wooden dowel, and how to put ordinary household supplies, such as freezer paper, plastic wrap, and paper clips, to new uses in the sewing room.

The Art of Copying

Clothing manufacturers often inspire home sewers with interesting styles. Learn how to copy garments by making your own pattern. The simple technique for duplicating a garment is called *rubbing off*, the same method used to rub off a coin or leaf with a soft lead pencil. Or learn how to copy design details from ready-to-wear, like tucks and mock front bands, using simplified construction methods.

Trade Secrets

This section of the book contains industry secrets shared by professional sewers and manufacturers. Learn new ways to solve old problems, such as how to sew perfectly straight rows of topstitching and how to attach facings at the top of a zipper, using a sewing machine instead of stitching by hand.

Discover faster and easier methods to sew flat-fell seams and tab plackets, and learn how to make custom Chinese ball buttons and frogs. This section also includes new uses for elastics and new ways to apply them.

Hooks and eyes are a basic sewing notion, but they can be used for more than just closures. Attach a metal eye to the shank of a button to make the shank more durable, or use it at the top of a skirt slit to keep the seam from tearing out. Also, learn how to reinforce the button closure on a skirt.

Designer Techniques

Learn how couture sewing techniques can make ruffles drape better, and learn tips for sewing bias-cut garments. Find out how designers use boning to get a smooth fit in evening dresses, and how they finish off silky garments with fast, neat bindings and narrow hems. Discover the secret for stitching beautiful tucks and darts in sheers, using single-thread machine sewing, and for creatively piecing striped fabric.

If you have problems sewing invisible stitches at hemlines, try the method for an invisible hanging hem. Or if you find that the hems pull out in coats, try the no-sag hem method.

Just for Fun

The last section of the book includes many ideas for the sheer enjoyment of sewing for fun. For example, use silk flowers as three-dimensional appliqués on garments or in shadow boxes. Or copy the look of lace by machine-embroidering on tulle, making custom lace designs for special garments. Even personalize stationery by perforating paper with the sewing machine.

Buttons can be decorative as well as functional. Learn how to make chrysanthemum buttons, and see some surprising new uses for purchased buttons, too.

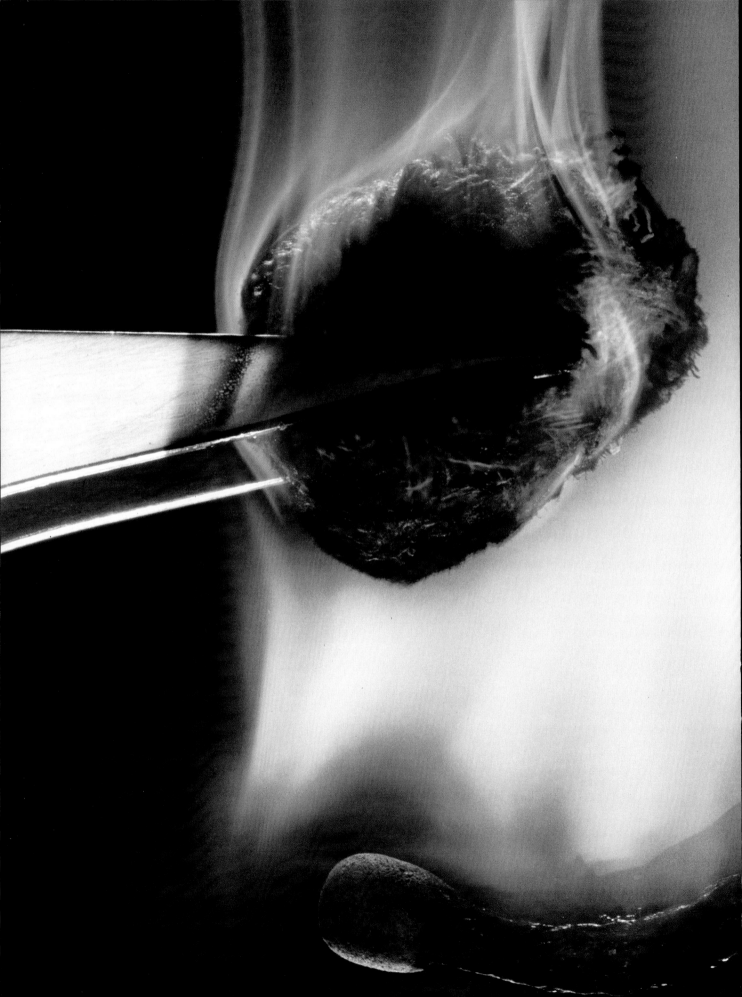

Sewing Room Secrets

Easy Organizing Ideas

Sewing time is productive and satisfying with careful planning. Make a list of all the items needed for a project and purchase them in one shopping trip.

If you already have a piece of fabric, measure the width and length before selecting a pattern. Also check the repeat of a print or plaid. Always take a sample of the fabric with you when selecting patterns and notions.

When choosing the fabric for a specific pattern, check the fabric recommendations on the pattern envelope. The first fabric listed is the one the designer selected for the original garment.

Hang garment pieces, with pattern attached, from a skirt hanger to prevent wrinkling. Attach bag containing notions and hang until ready to use.

Place transparent tape on the wrong side of each garment piece, for quick identification after pattern is removed.

Place pattern, thread, buttons, and other notions for a project in a large, clear, self-closing plastic bag. Wind several bobbins with thread to match the fabric to avoid interruptions during construction.

Cut a slit in a fabric swatch and take swatch with you when shopping for buttons. Check the size and color of button against fabric by sliding the still-carded button through the slit in the swatch.

Unorganized fabrics become wrinkled. It is also difficult to find the fabric you are looking for.

Organized fabrics may be stored in clear plastic boxes according to fabric type or color for quick identification.

Organizing & Using Your Fabric Stash

An organized fabric collection eliminates the problem of forgotten fabric and helps you to use what you have to its best advantage. Make a note of the length, width, fiber content, pattern repeat in inches, care method, date, and place of purchase on a card. Pin the card to the selvage with a small safety pin.

You may want to divide the fabrics according to categories such as color, fiber content, or care method. Or divide them according to use; for example, all silky blouse-weights in one section and all heavy coatings in another.

How you decide to store your fabric stash depends on the space available. If you have closet space, fabrics can be folded and stacked on shelves or clipped to hangers. Drawer space works well to store folded fabric. Clear plastic boxes stacked on open shelves in your sewing area keep your fabric visible.

If you have purchased fabric that you are not planning to use right away, pretreat or launder it so it is ready to sew. You may want to finish the raw edges before laundering to prevent raveling. Before laundering, place a small safety pin in the selvage on the right side of the fabric. When the fabric is taken from the fabric stash, the right side can be found quickly.

When you are not sure which side of the fabric is the right side, remember cottons and linens are usually folded onto the bolt wrong sides together. Wool fabrics are usually folded with right sides together or rolled on a tube, wrong side out. If you are still not sure, look for pinholes in the selvage; pins are usually inserted from the wrong side during manufacturing.

Swatching Your Fabric Stash

Swatch file. Cut swatch of each fabric in your fabric stash. Staple to index cards and secure cards with a metal ring. Update swatch file as fabrics are used and added.

Purse-size notebook. Cut swatch of each fabric in your fabric stash, and place in a notebook for handy reference when shopping. Update notebook as fabrics are used and added.

Using Short Yardages

Sometimes you find a pattern that would be perfect for one of the fabrics in your fabric stash, but there is not quite enough yardage to make the garment. There are several ways to solve this problem. You may be able to shorten the finished length of the garment on the pattern tissue. Or you could change from long to short sleeves. When cutting plain-weave fabrics, you can place some pattern pieces on the crosswise grain to help fit them on the fabric.

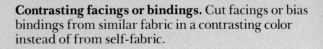

Contrasting facings or bindings. Cut facings or bias bindings from similar fabric in a contrasting color instead of from self-fabric.

14

Piecing. Cut large pattern sections into smaller sections; several small pieces may fit better on your fabric than one large piece. Add seam allowances where patterns are cut apart, and match grainlines. Topstitching can be used to emphasize design lines.

Contrasting details. Use contrasting fabric for details such as front bands, cuffs, and lapels. Mix solid colors with patterned fabrics, for a coordinated look. Or use fabrics such as cotton velveteen, stable knits, or leather.

Color blocking. Combine two or more similar fabrics in one garment. Cut the pattern apart at chosen design lines, add seam allowances, and stitch pieces together. Topstitch to add detail.

Testing Fabric for Fiber Content

It is important to know the fiber content of fabric if you have allergies, and also to determine its care method. The appearance and feel of a fabric give you clues to its fiber content. Linens and cottons, for example, tend to wrinkle easily when crushed, and silks feel soapy or gummy to the touch.

The burn test is a way of distinguishing between natural and synthetic fibers. Natural fibers burn and char, leaving an ash; synthetic fibers melt, producing a hard bead. All cotton, linen, and rayon fibers are cellulose, and tend to burn in the same way. Wool and silk fibers are protein, and burn in the same way.

Some fabrics may be treated with sizing, dyes, and finishes that alter the flammability of fibers.

Separate crosswise and lengthwise yarns of a small woven scrap, or unravel a knit scrap. Differences in the luster, twist, and color of the fibers indicate that the fabric may be a blend. Blends will burn like the predominant fiber in the fabric, but they cannot be identified by a burn test.

To conduct the burn test, roll the yarns into a small ball and hold it with tweezers or tongs as you burn it in a fireproof container.

Tests to Determine Fiber Content

Cotton, linen, and rayon. Fibers burn vigorously, with an afterglow. They burn with the odor of burning paper and leave a soft, gray ash.

Wool and silk. Fibers burn slowly and char, curling away from flame. They sometimes burn only while in the flame. They burn with the odor of burning hair or feathers and leave a crushable ash.

Polyester, nylon, and other synthetics. Fibers burn and melt only while in the flame, or shortly after being removed. They burn with a chemical odor and leave a hard bead.

Acetate and acrylic. Fibers burn and melt while in the flame and after being removed. They leave a hard bead. Test for acetate by placing fabric scrap in acetone nail polish remover; acetate will dissolve.

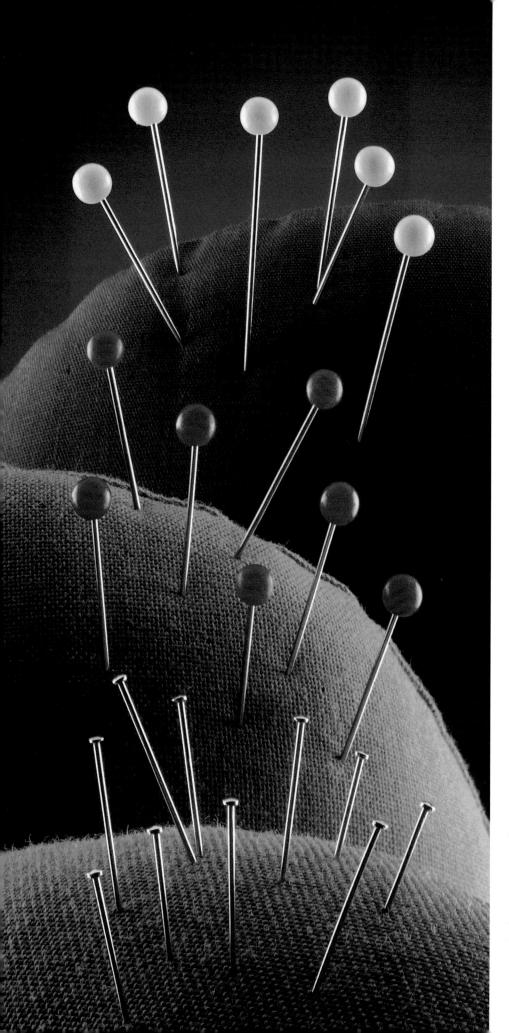

Selecting Pins

Pins are manufactured to standard lengths and wire diameters. The finest are silk pins, 0.50 mm in diameter; the coarsest are T-pins, 1.16 mm in diameter. Length is measured in sixteenths of an inch. A size 16 pin is $^{16}/_{16}$" or 1" (2.5 cm) long; a size 20 is $^{20}/_{16}$" or 1¼" (3.2 cm) long. The most common is a 17 dressmaker pin.

Most pins are made of brass, nickel-plated steel, or stainless steel. Brass pins do not stick to a magnetic pincushion, and they do not rust.

To organize pins, separate them by size and type on different-colored pincushions. Dull, bent, or nicked pins should be discarded, because they can damage fabric. Never sew over pins, because they can scratch the needle plate or the bottom of the presser foot, or damage the needle.

Types of Pins

1) Dressmaker pins are for all-purpose general sewing, but are not used for fine, silky fabrics. They are made from medium-size wire of brass, nickel-plated steel, or stainless steel and can have ball or sharp points. They are available in sizes 17, 1¹⁄₁₆" (2.5 cm), and 20, 1¼" (3.2 cm), with regular, glass, or plastic heads.

2) Silk pins work well for fine silk and synthetic fabrics; the holes they make are small and vanish quickly. They are made from fine wire and are available in sizes 17, 1¹⁄₁₆" (2.5 cm), and 20, 1¼" (3.2 cm).

3) Ballpoint pins are designed specifically for knit fabrics, to slide between fibers rather than pierce them. They are available in size 17, 1¹⁄₁₆" (2.5 cm)

4) Pleating pins are designed for lightweight to mediumweight woven and knit fabrics. They are fine pins of medium length and have ball points. They are available in size 16, 1" (2.5 cm).

5) Quilting pins are used for bulky layers. They are extra long with a narrow shaft and are available in size 28, 1¾" (4.5 cm), with regular or glass heads.

6) T-pins are used for crafts or for pinning heavy fabrics to dress forms. They are long pins made of heavy wire and are available in sizes 20, 1¼" (3.2 cm), and 28, 1¾" (4.5 cm).

7) Sequin pins are primarily used for pinning sequins and beads to Styrofoam®. They are short and are available in sizes 8, ½" (1.3 cm), and 12, ¾" (2 cm) with a regular head.

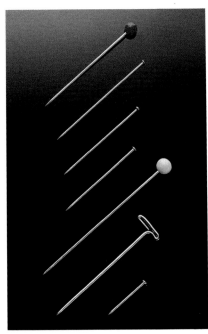

Pins are shown actual size.

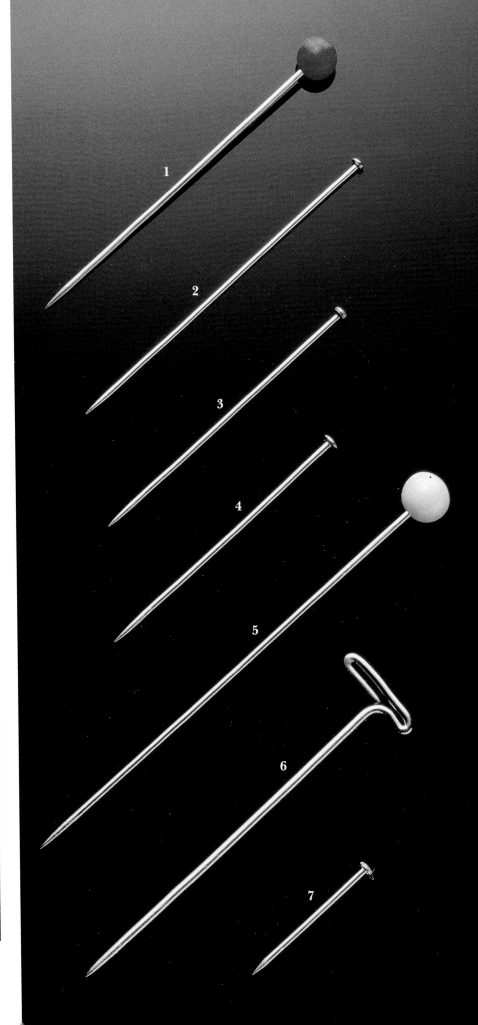

1

2

3

4

5

6

7

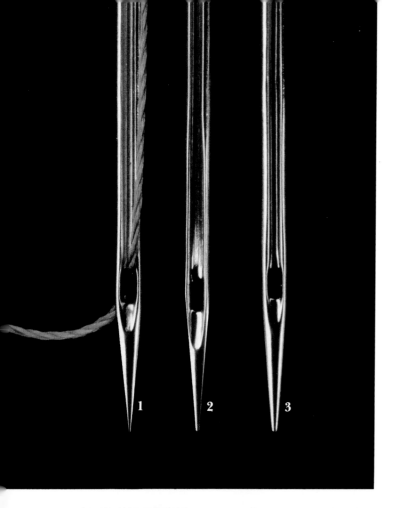

Selecting Machine Needles

The European sizing system for sewing machine needles is numbered from 60 to 120, based on the diameter of the needle; the American system is numbered from 8 to 21. This sizing system does not include industrial needles.

Most packages have both numbers to avoid confusion, such as 60/8 and 100/16. A size 60/8 needle is .6 mm, and a 100/16 is 1 mm in diameter. The smaller the number, the finer the needle.

1) Sharps are used for all woven fabrics, particularly those of heavy weight and dense weave. They are good for topstitching, because they have a sharp point for penetrating thread. Sizes range from 60/8 to 120/20.

2) Universal needles are used for all-purpose sewing; the larger sizes are used for topstitching. The slightly rounded tip penetrates fabrics by dividing the threads. Sizes range from 60/8 to 120/20.

3) Ballpoint needles are used for sewing on knits; the rounded tip allows the needle to pass between threads instead of penetrating them. Sizes range from 60/8 to 100/16.

Leather needles cut smoothly through leather without tearing it or causing skipped stitches. They are not recommended for synthetic suedes. They are wedge-shaped, with cutting points. Sizes range from 90/14 to 110/18.

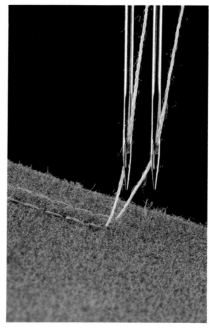

Twin needles, or double needles, are used for decorative sewing, topstitching, and pin tucks. Two needles are mounted on a single shank. Sizes range from 80/12 to 90/14 in widths 1.8 mm to 4.0 mm. A size 75/11 stretch twin needle is 4.0 mm in width.

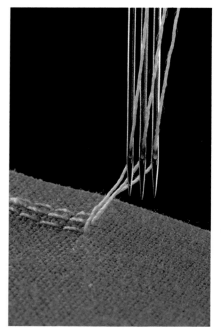

Triple needles are designed for decorative straight stitching with fine thread, but are not for use on heavy fabrics or multiple layers. Three needles are mounted close together on the same shank. Sizes range from 80/12, 2.5 mm width, to 90/14, 3.0 mm width.

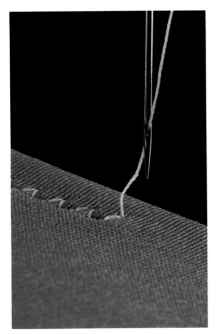

Stretch needles, like ballpoint needles, are designed to prevent skipped stitches on stretch fabric. Sizes range from 75/11 to 90/14.

Jeans needles, or denim needles, are for sewing tightly woven fabrics and fabrics with a heavy finish; they resist deflection because they have acute rounded points, stiff shafts, and slender eyes. Sizes range from 90/14 to 110/18.

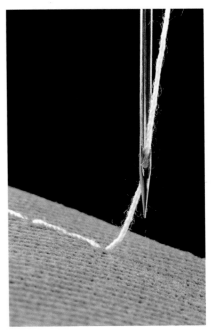

Topstitching needles have large eyes to accommodate heavier threads, such as topstitching thread, without skipping stitches or stripping thread. Sizes range from 80/12 to 110/18.

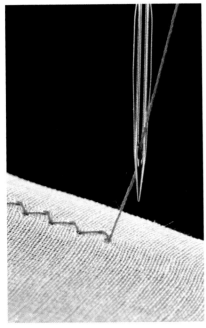

Wing needles are designed for decorative hemstitching. They push threads apart, creating a hole in crisp fabrics, such as linen. The shafts are like two wings projecting from either side of the eye. Sizes range from 100/16 to 120/20.

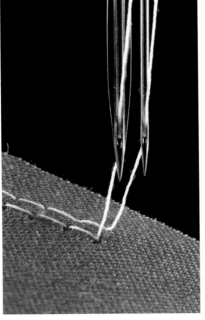

Double-wing needles are used for decorative sewing or for machine heirloom sewing. Two needles are mounted on the same shank; the standard needle makes a small hole and the wing needle does hemstitching. They are available in size 100/16 only.

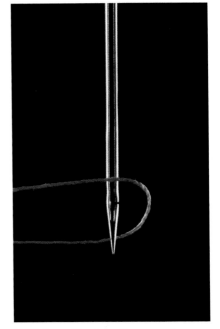

Self-threading needles, or calyx-eye needles, are used by people who have difficulty threading needles. A slot is cut on a slant into the eye so thread can slide down the shaft until it slips into the eye. They are used for sewing on mediumweight fabrics. Sizes range from 80/11 to 100/16.

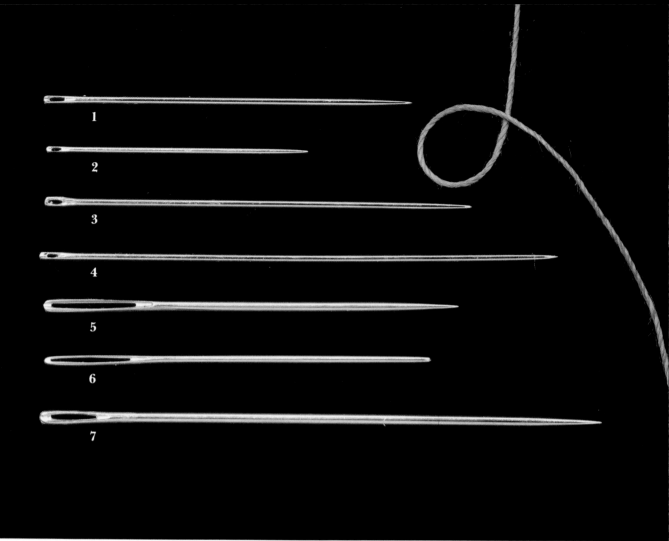

Selecting Hand Needles

In choosing a needle for a specific job, consider the type of thread and fabric you will be using. Use the finest needle that will accommodate the thread or yarn desired for sewing. The finer or more sheer the fabric, the more sharp and slender the needle should be. Most needles are numbered according to two different scales, either 1 to 15 or 13 to 26. In each scale, the smaller the number, the longer and thicker the needle. Some needles have ballpoint tips for use in sewing knit fabrics.

Platinum-plated needles are stainless steel, thinly coated with platinum to reduce drag and friction as the needle slides through the fabric. Platinum needles shorten sewing time and are resistant to body oils and acids, eliminating needle stains. Although any type of needle can be platinum-plated, the most common ones are betweens, crewel, and darning needles.

1) Sharps are for all-purpose sewing. They are medium-length needles with small, rounded eyes. Sizes range from 1 to 12.

2) Betweens are for detailed handwork and quilting. They are short needles with small, rounded eyes. Sizes range from 1 to 12.

3) Ballpoint needles are for all-purpose sewing on knits. They have a special tip that enables the needle to slide between knit threads. Sizes range from 1 to 10.

4) Milliners needles are for basting, gathering, and millinery work. They are long and fine with small, rounded eyes. Sizes range from 1 to 10 and 15 to 18.

5) Chenille needles are for heavy embroidery on tightly woven fabrics. They are short and thick with large eyes and sharp points. Sizes range from 13 to 24.

6) Tapestry needles are for embroidery on loosely woven fabrics and are good for small children learning to sew. They are short needles with blunt tips and long eyes to accommodate multiple strands of thread. Sizes range from 13 to 26.

7) Darners are for making repairs with multiple strands of thread, yarn, or floss. The length of the needle is helpful in spanning the hole being darned. They are coarse with large eyes. Sizes range from 1 to 9 and 14 to 18.

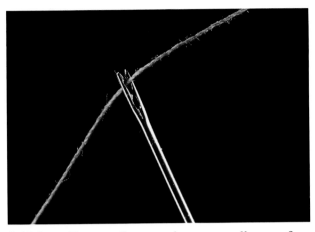

Self-threading needles, or calyx-eye needles, are for general sewing by people who have difficulty threading needles. These needles have two eyes; to thread the needle, snap the thread into the top eye. Sizes range from 4 to 8.

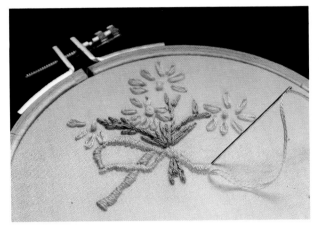

Embroidery needles, or crewel needles, are of medium length and have long, oval eyes to accommodate yarn or several strands of embroidery floss. Sizes range from 1 to 10.

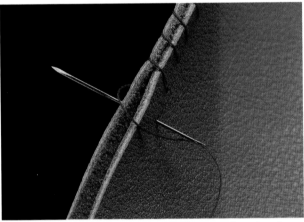

Leather needles, or glovers needles, are for piercing leather, synthetic suedes, and plastic without tearing holes. They are long and sturdy with sharp, tapered, triangular tips. Sizes range from 1 to 8.

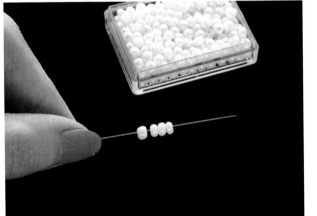

Beading needles are for picking up several beads or seed pearls at a time before attaching to project. They are long and fine with small, round eyes. Sizes range from 10 to 15.

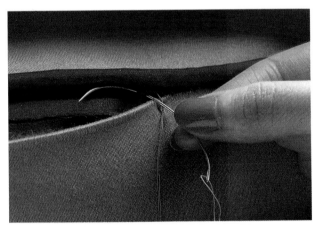

Upholstery needles are for sewing on upholstered furniture. They are strong curved or straight needles with large eyes to accommodate heavy upholstery thread. Curved needles range from 2" (5 cm) to 8" (20.5 cm); straight, from 4" (10 cm) to 16" (40.5 cm).

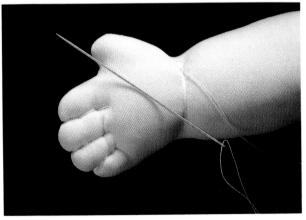

Doll needles, or soft-sculpture needles, are for stitching the body and facial features of a cloth-bodied doll. They are of medium weight with long eyes. Lengths range from 3½" (9 cm) to 6" (15 cm).

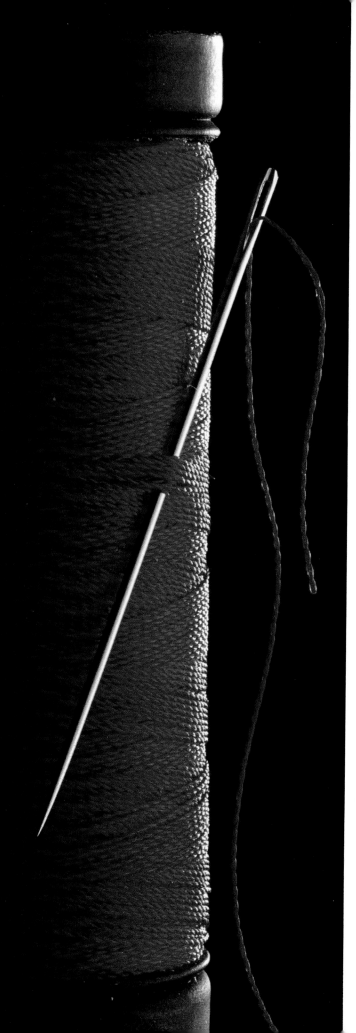

Thread Secrets

Thread is an important part of a garment. Skipped stitches, puckered seams, and thread breakage can often be eliminated by the correct thread choice.

Cotton thread sews well and dyes readily. A good-quality mercerized cotton thread has more strength and less lint than inexpensive cotton thread. Polyester thread provides strength, stretchability, and abrasion-resistance. Cotton-wrapped polyester thread combines the good qualities of both fibers; it sews like cotton and has the strength of polyester.

Monofilament nylon thread blends with the fabric so well that it is almost invisible. Lightweight nylon thread is not strong enough for areas of stress, but can be used for hems and seam finishes. Woolly nylon thread is dyed in many colors and is soft, comfortable, and strong.

Generally, thread that is made from natural fibers, such as cotton, is used for sewing fabrics of natural fiber content; thread that is made from synthetic fibers, such as polyester or nylon, is used for sewing synthetics. Cotton-wrapped polyester thread can be used for sewing all fabrics.

Thread quality. A good-quality thread **(a)** is smooth and feeds evenly. A poor-quality thread **(b)** has thick and thin areas that restrict the smooth flow, causing excessive lint and strip-back. Hold light thread against dark fabric and dark thread against light fabric to check the quality.

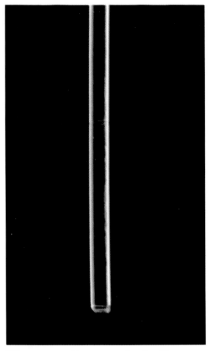

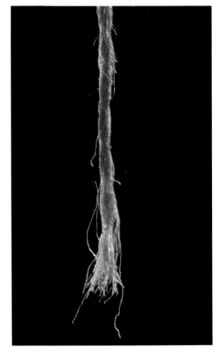

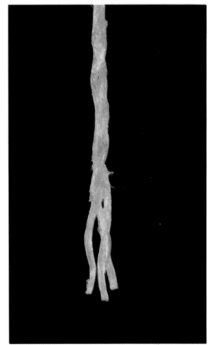

Filament refers to a single fiber of indefinite length up to several miles long. Monofilament nylon thread is a single filament; woolly nylon thread is made from several filaments loosely twisted together.

Staple refers to the length of the fibers spun together to form the thread. Threads may be long or short staple; use long-staple thread for smooth, trouble-free sewing.

Ply refers to the number of strands that are twisted together to form the thread. Three-ply thread is used for general-purpose sewing. Two-ply thread is extra fine and is used for embroidery and machine darning.

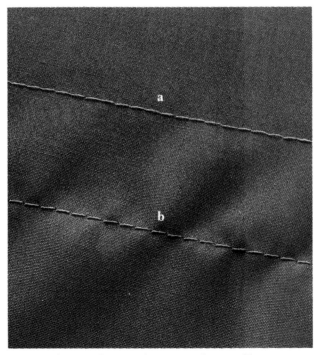

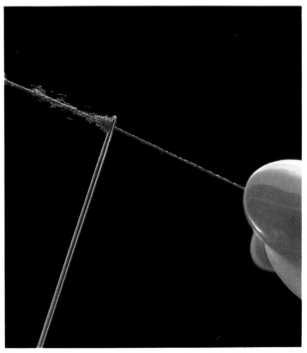

Preventing puckers. Polyester and monofilament nylon threads are strong and abrasion-resistant, with the ability to stretch, so they work especially well on stretch fabrics. Hold fabric taut when stitching the seams to prevent seams that are flat and smooth immediately after they are sewn **(a)** from puckering a day or two later **(b).**

Preventing strip-back. Use good-quality thread and the correct size needle to prevent strip-back, frayed thread that bunches up at the eye of the needle. Uneven or linty thread strips back, causing it to break. Strip-back also occurs if thread is abraded by rough areas on the sewing machine or by a needle that has an eye too small for the thread.

Making Your Own Pressing Aids

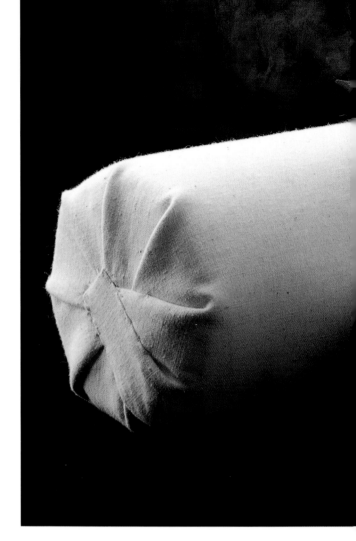

Use of the proper pressing equipment can help you produce a professionally finished garment; however, this does not require spending a lot of money. Some everyday household items can be used for making pressing equipment.

A padded seam roll holds steam and can be made to any length. Wrap a 1" (2.5 cm) dowel tightly with layers of wool fabric, and cover the wool with muslin.

A magazine, rolled tightly and placed inside a muslin tube, expands to fit the tube, making a firm seam roll.

Wooden dowels of various diameters are handy aids for pressing seams open. The curved surface of a dowel prevents seam edges from being touched by the iron, eliminating show-through on the right side of the garment.

How to Make a Padded Seam Roll

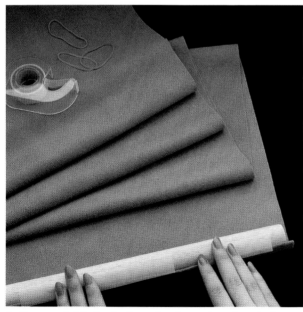

1) Cut wool fabric the length of wooden dowel plus ½" (1.3 cm). Fasten wool fabric with tape or staples to 1" (2.5 cm) dowel; wrap tightly to desired diameter. Hold in place with rubber bands; whipstitch.

2) Cut muslin the length of dowel plus allowance for finishing ends. Wrap roll tightly with muslin. Turn under raw edge. Hold in place with rubber bands; slipstitch edge and ends securely.

Two Ways to Use Dowels for Pressing Seams

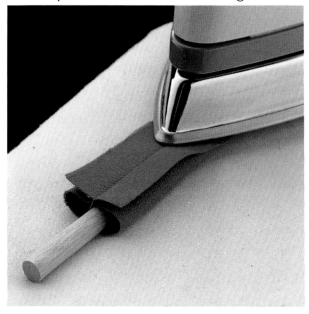

Small dowel. Use a ⅜" (1 cm) diameter wooden dowel to press seams open in hard-to-reach places, such as cuffs, straps, and the ends of waistbands.

Large dowel. Use 1" (2.5 cm) diameter wooden dowel to press seams open without leaving imprint of seam on the right side of fabric.

Using Freezer Paper as a Stitching Guide

Freezer paper can be used as a press-on stitching guide where accurate stitching is important. Stitch along the edge of the freezer paper and peel it away when finished.

Freezer paper works well for making quilting templates. Draw the design on the flat, unshiny side of the paper,

making mirror images of letters and numbers. It will help in assembling the quilt if you mark the color on the template and number the pieces sequentially. Make a duplicate master pattern to use as a reference.

How to Use Freezer Paper

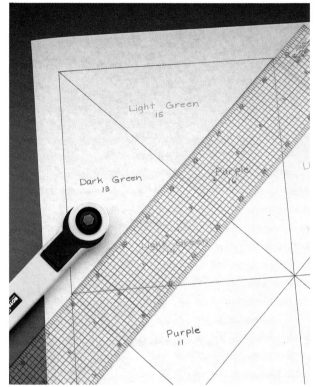

1) Cut quilting templates from design that is drawn, color-coded, and numbered on freezer paper.

2) Press templates, shiny side down, on wrong side of fabric, using dry iron on cotton setting. Cut fabric, adding ¼" (6 mm) seam allowances.

3) Stitch pieces together to form quilt block, using template as a stitching guide. Peel off template, and reuse.

For garment details. Stitch a collar, cuff, pocket, or other detail, using a freezer paper pattern pressed on the wrong side of the fabric as a stitching guide.

Reinforcing Patterns with Plastic Film

Tissue patterns that are used repeatedly will eventually wear out. A good way to preserve them and increase their durability is to use plastic film as an adhesive between the pattern and a sheet of tissue paper. Plastic wrap or dry-cleaning bags work well. The plastic wrap that is manufactured for use in microwave ovens may not adhere.

The plastic is sandwiched between the tissue paper backing and the pattern, and then pressed. As a precaution against getting melted plastic on the hot iron, cover the exposed plastic with another layer of tissue paper.

The fused pattern can be stored by clipping it to a skirt hanger or by rolling it loosely.

How to Fuse a Pattern with Plastic Film

Smooth pattern and tissue paper, using a warm, dry iron. Place tissue paper, cut larger than pattern, on ironing board; cover with plastic film. Place pattern, printed side up, on plastic. Cover exposed plastic with tissue paper.

Press slowly over pattern, using dry iron at cotton setting. Turn over, and press again. Check to see that all areas have adhered. When cool, trim excess tissue paper and plastic film.

Holding Fabrics without Pins

Some fabrics are so bulky or heavy in texture that they are difficult to secure with pins. When sewing on leather, vinyl, synthetic suede, synthetic fur, upholstery fabric, and quilted fabric, use items such as paper clips, binder clips, clothespins, and tape to securely hold seams together before stitching.

The clips or clothespins must be removed immediately before they reach the presser foot, to allow for stitching while the rest of the seam is held in place.

Two Ways to Hold Fabrics without Pins

Hold layers of dense, heavy, or bulky fabric in place with binder clips to prevent shifting while stitching.

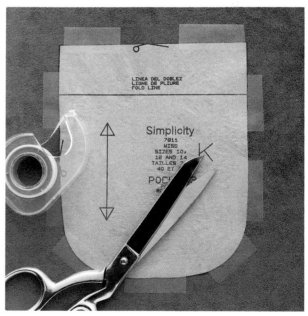

Tape pattern to fabric that can be damaged by pins. Cut one layer at a time for accuracy.

Solving Sewing Room Mishaps

While you are constructing a garment, few things are as annoying as accidentally staining or scorching the fabric. No matter how careful you are, accidents do happen, but some can be remedied. Always test the spot treatment on a scrap of self-fabric or on a hidden section of the garment, such as a seam allowance, facing, or hem.

Tips for Solving Mishaps

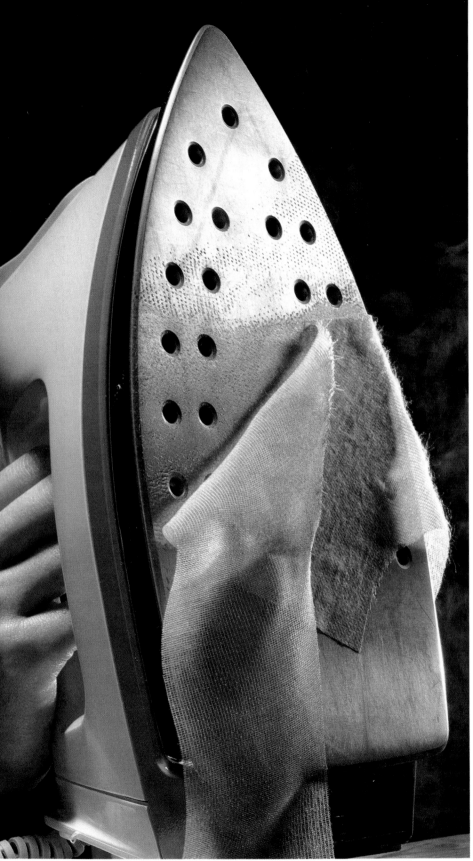

Fusible resins. Remove resins from iron soleplate using a commercial iron cleaner, or for a small amount of fusible resin, use a crumpled ball of wax paper. To remove fusible resins from fabric, use denatured alcohol.

Tracing-paper marks. Blot with a cotton ball dampened with dry-cleaning solvent, and launder in water as hot as fabric can stand.

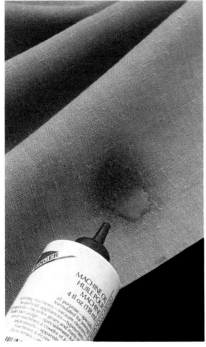

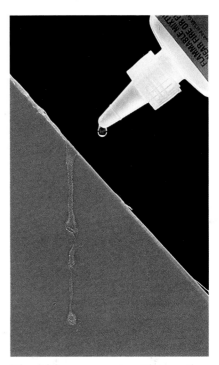

Sewing machine oil. Blot with cotton ball dampened with dry-cleaning solvent on all fabrics. Or, for a washable fabric, use an oil-based laundry pretreatment or liquid laundry detergent applied directly to the stain.

Scorch. Blot scorch with a cotton ball dampened with 3% hydrogen peroxide. Or cover the scorch with peroxide-saturated cloth; then cover with dry cloth, and press with iron as hot as fabric can stand. Rinse fabric thoroughly.

Liquid fray preventer. Blot gently with a cotton ball dampened with denatured alcohol. Once liquid fray preventer dries, the stain takes longer to remove.

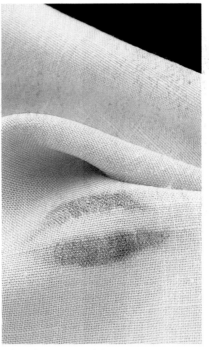

Water-soluble marking pen. Blot with a cotton ball dampened with 3% hydrogen peroxide any mark that has been pressed with a hot iron. Rinse fabric thoroughly.

Lipstick. Rub stick stain remover, liquid laundry detergent, or oil-based laundry pretreatment into stain; launder. Use dry-cleaning solvent on nonwashable fabric.

Blood. Wash in cold water. Or blot with fabric scrap moistened with your own saliva, which contains the same enzymes as your blood; this helps to remove stain. For stubborn stains, use an enzyme presoak.

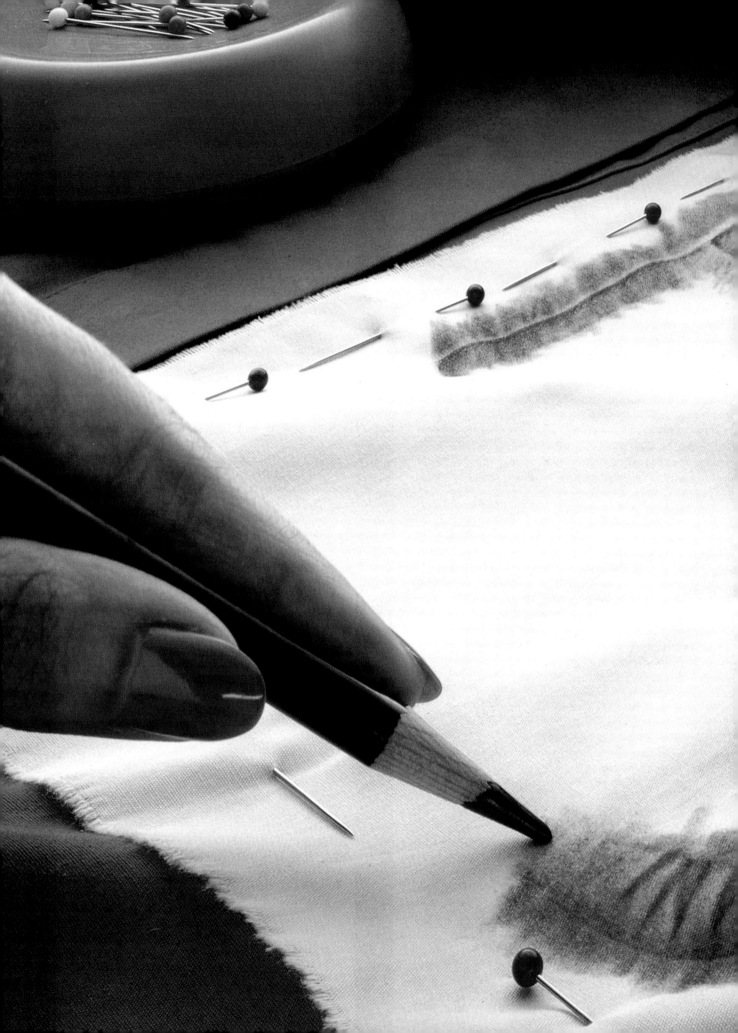

The Art of Copying

The Rub-off Technique

Perhaps your favorite garment is showing wear, or you want the good fit or style of a certain garment transferred to another fabric. You can copy the garment without taking it apart to make a pattern, using a technique called *rubbing off*. This technique is similar to the way impressions of coins or leaves are made, using a soft lead pencil.

To copy each garment section, a piece of muslin is placed over the outside of the garment, then pinned and smoothed from the center to the seamlines. Seamlines and garment details are copied onto the muslin by rubbing over them with a soft lead pencil.

Examine the garment to see how it was constructed, because you will not have instructions for the pattern you rub off. Also check to see where interfacing is used on the original garment.

You may want to make a trial garment in an inexpensive fabric to test the muslin pattern. Or use the muslin pieces themselves, basted together, for a trial fitting. Then make any necessary adjustments on the muslin before sewing the new garment.

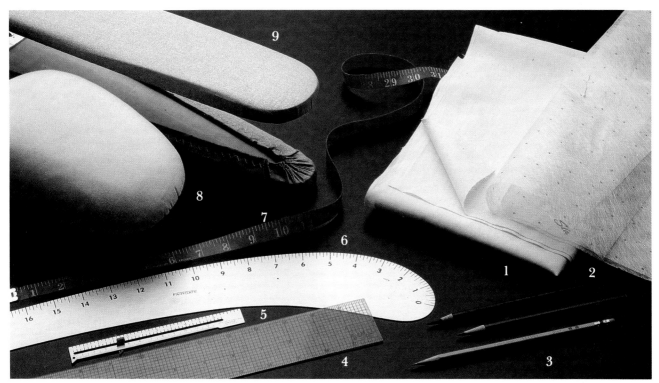

Equipment. Lightweight muslin (**1**) is used as the tracing material; pattern tracing paper (**2**), a thin, translucent nonwoven fabric with or without grid marks, may be used instead of muslin. A soft lead pencil (**3**) is used for marking the tracing material.

Measuring tools include 2" × 18" (5 × 46 cm) transparent ruler (**4**), seam gauge (**5**), curved ruler (**6**), and measuring tape (**7**). A tailor's ham (**8**) is needed for copying shaped areas, and a sleeve board (**9**) for copying a set-in sleeve.

Rub-off Guidelines

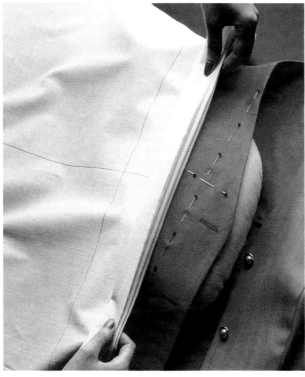

Mark grainlines on garment and muslin. Cover garment section with the muslin, matching grainlines.

Smooth layers of garment and muslin. Rub or trace along details such as buttonholes and seamlines, using a soft lead pencil, to make a pattern.

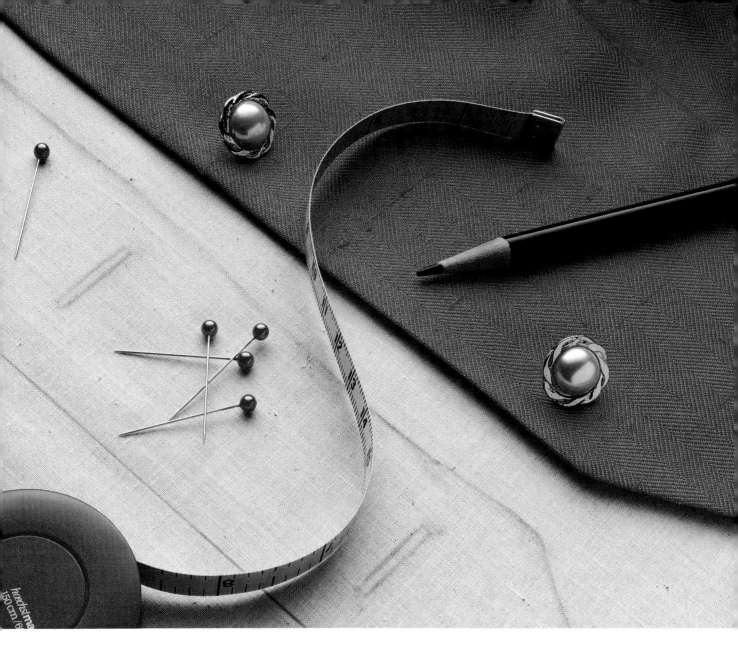

Rubbing Off a Garment

Before you begin to copy a garment, clean and press it to eliminate any wearing distortions. Then mark the lengthwise grainlines on each garment section. It is helpful to also mark the crosswise grainlines, especially if you are copying garment sections that have gathers, tucks, or darts. If the grainline of the original garment is not marked accurately, the new garment may not drape the same way.

Mark the grainlines on a piece of muslin, and place it over the garment section. Pin the muslin to the garment, matching grainlines, and smooth the layers as you work from the center out to the seamlines. Place pins close together to prevent the fabric from shifting. To mark the seamlines on the muslin, rub over the seamlines or trace along them with a soft lead pencil.

After rubbing off all the garment sections, measure the dimensions of the muslin pattern pieces and

compare them to the garment to check the accuracy of the pattern. Also measure the seamlines that are to be sewn together; they should be the same length, unless they have ease, tucks, or gathers. Draw over the traced lines with a straightedge or curved ruler to create smooth, even lines; this is called *trueing*. Add seam allowances, and label each pattern piece with the name of the garment section and the number of pieces to cut.

It is only necessary to copy the right or left garment sections of a symmetrical garment, or to copy half of any large symmetrical piece that will be placed on the fold when cutting out the new garment.

Detailed instructions given here are for copying basic garment sections that can be laid flat. To copy a set-in sleeve, see pages 42 and 43. To copy rectangular pieces and details that have fullness, such as elasticized areas, gathers, darts, and tucks, see pages 44 to 47.

How to Rub Off a Garment

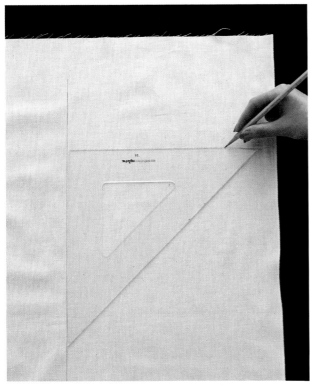

1) Cut a piece of muslin larger than each garment section, allowing extra length and width for hem and seam allowances. Mark grainlines on each piece.

2) Mark grainlines on each garment section by pinning, or by basting along grainlines with contrasting thread.

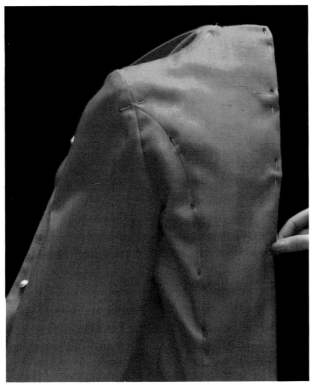

3) Fold garment section in half on center back or center front foldline, if garment section will be cut out on a fold. Baste on foldline.

4) Place pins across seamlines where notches are desired, such as at armholes and areas that are eased or gathered.

(continued on next page)

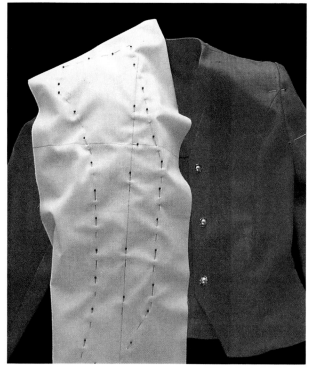

5) Place muslin over garment section, matching grainlines; pin. Smooth fabrics, pinning across garment and hem areas as necessary to hold muslin and garment in place. Pin parallel to seamlines.

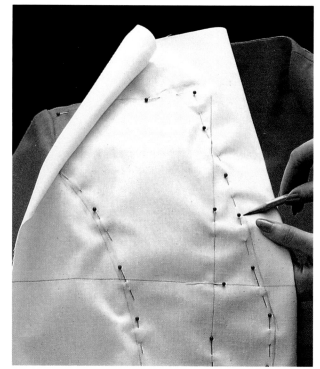

6) Rub over seamlines, using soft lead pencil, to transfer them to muslin; place pins on seamline, if necessary, to define the line. Rub over details, such as buttonholes and pockets, to mark placement; rub over pins to mark notches. Remove muslin.

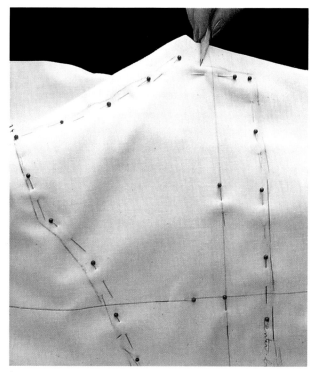

7) Repeat steps to copy other garment sections, rubbing off only half of any garment section that will be cut out on a fold, page 39, step 3. Mark foldline on muslin.

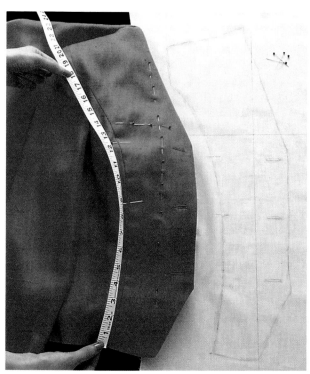

8) Compare length of seams and dimensions of all muslin garment sections to those of garment; make necessary adjustments.

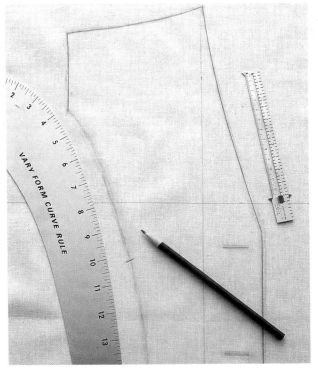

9) True seamlines of all garment sections; use a ruler to draw straight seamlines or a curved ruler to draw curved lines.

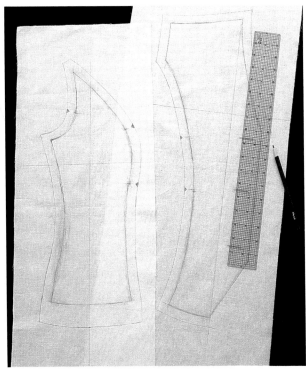

10) Add seam allowances and hem allowances.

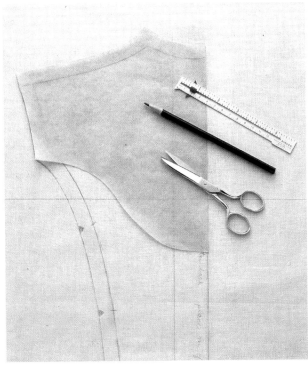

11) Copy facings, using rub-off method. Or use muslin pieces to draw facing patterns.

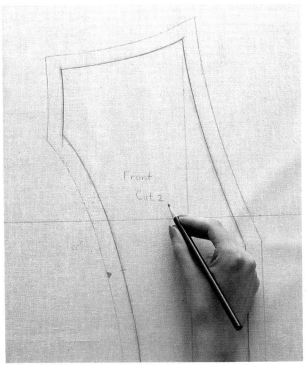

12) Label muslin pieces with name of garment section and number of pieces to cut.

Rubbing Off a Sleeve

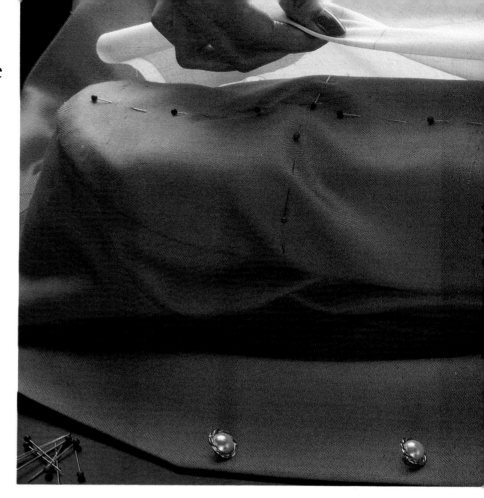

To make an accurate pattern for a set-in sleeve, place the sleeve over a sleeve board so the muslin can be draped around it and pinned. A tailor's ham or the end of a sleeve board is used to shape the sleeve cap.

For a smooth set-in sleeve, the seamline of the sleeve cap should be 1" to 1½" (2.5 to 3.8 cm) larger than the armhole seamline. Since the sleeve cap can be easily flattened in the rubbing process, it may be necessary to add more ease by raising the seamline of the sleeve cap in an even curve, tapering to the seamline in the notch area.

How to Rub Off a Sleeve

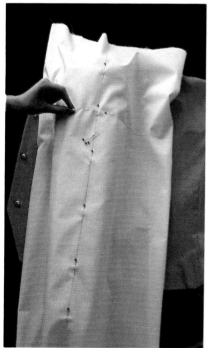

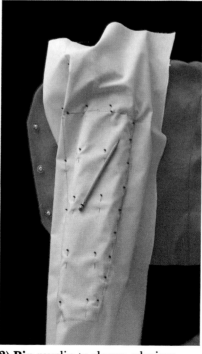

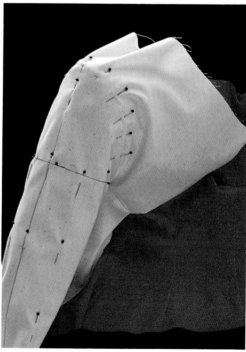

1) Mark lengthwise grainlines on sleeve and muslin; mark crosswise grainline across sleeve cap and on muslin. Working on a sleeve board, match grainlines of sleeve and muslin; pin.

2) Pin muslin to sleeve, placing rows of pins 2" to 3" (5 to 7.5 cm) apart and keeping layers smooth; do not pin sleeve cap area. Rub off sleeve seams and lower edge.

3) Place sleeve cap over tailor's ham or end of sleeve board. Shape and ease muslin to duplicate ease in sleeve cap; pin in place.

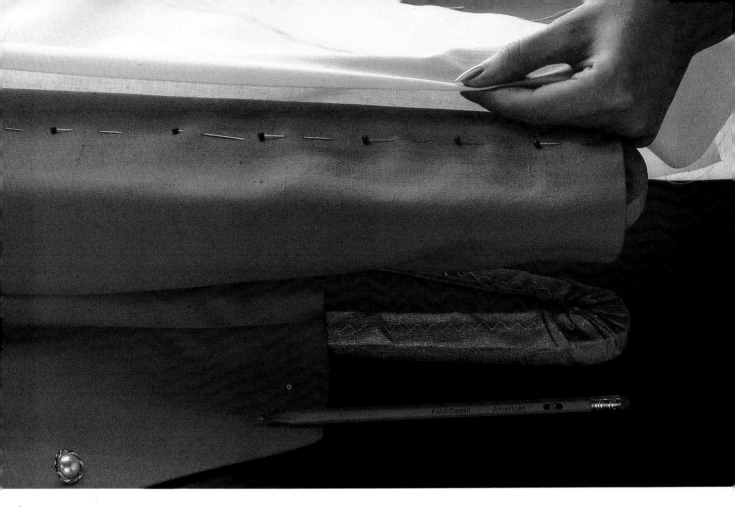

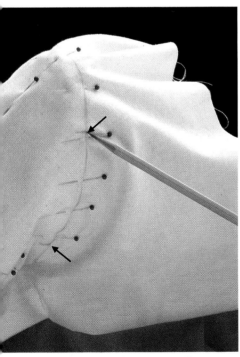

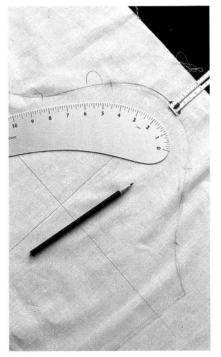

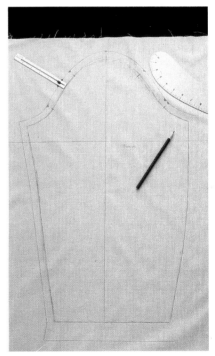

4) Rub off sleeve cap seamline; mark notches to correspond to seamlines and notch areas (arrows). Remove pins and muslin.

5) Compare measurement of armhole and sleeve cap seamline. If more ease is needed, raise sleeve cap. For each ¼" (6 mm) the sleeve cap is raised, ½" (1.3 cm) ease is added between notches.

6) Compare dimensions of muslin pattern to sleeve; make necessary adjustments. True seamlines. Add seam and hem allowances. Label muslin pattern.

Copying Other Details

When copying rectangular pieces, such as waistbands, cuffs, and pocket flaps, it is easier to measure them than to rub them off; draw the new patterns on tissue, according to the measurements. This also allows you to improve on the outline of the garment details, since the edges of already constructed garments may not be perfectly straight.

When copying areas that are shaped, mark and match both the lengthwise and crosswise grainlines of the garment and muslin. In an elasticized area, you can stretch the elastic until the garment is flat and smooth, and then rub off each garment section.

It may be easier to fold the garment in half on the center back or center front if the garment section will be cut on the fold.

Garment sections cannot be smoothed flat if they have darts or seams that are gathered or eased, so special methods are used to copy them.

The exact shape and size of darts can be copied, using the rub-off technique, even if the darts have been trimmed. The same method used for copying darts is used for short, shaped pleats, such as those at a yoke or waistband.

How to Copy Rectangular Pieces on a Garment

1) Measure length and width of rectangular garment detail to be copied.

2) Draw pattern according to measurements. Mark grainline on pattern to correspond to garment. Add seam allowances.

How to Copy Elasticized Areas on a Garment

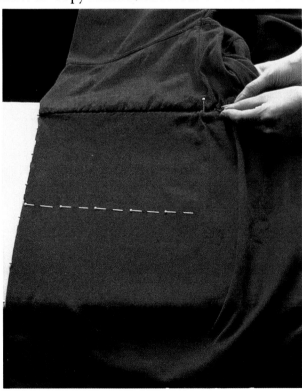

1) Mark grainlines of garment and muslin. Stretch elastic to smooth garment; pin to padded surface.

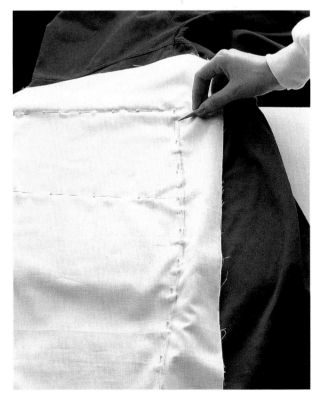

2) Pin muslin to garment, matching grainlines. Rub off and true seamlines. Add seam allowances.

How to Rub Off a Garment Section with a Dart

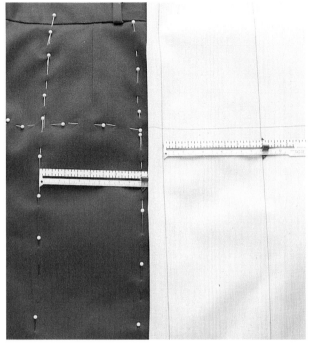

1) Mark lengthwise grainline on each side of dart; if there is more than one dart, also mark lengthwise grainline between darts. Mark crosswise grainline beyond points of darts. Mark grainlines on muslin as on garment, with lengthwise rows the same distance apart as on garment.

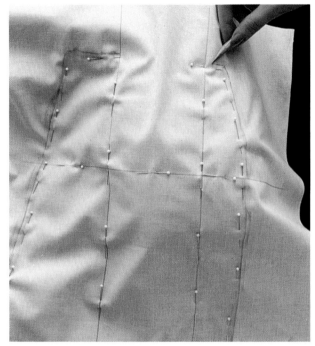

2) Match grainlines of garment section and muslin. Over a tailor's ham, rub off seamlines, except for dart area between grainlines.

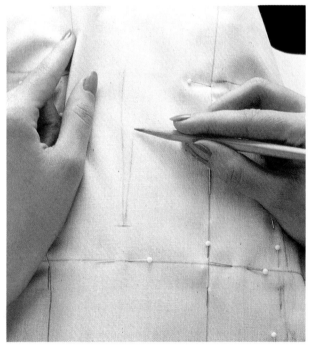

3) Smooth fabric from each grainline on either side of dart toward dart, one side at a time, and rub off stitching lines. Mark across point of dart.

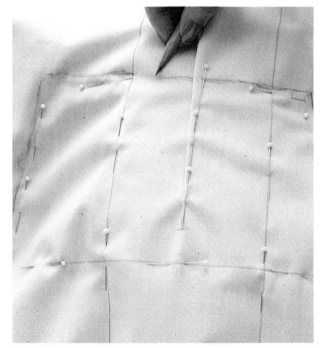

4) Pin dart along stitching lines; fold dart toward center, or down. Check to see that muslin lies smooth over garment. Rub off remaining seamline. Remove from tailor's ham.

5) Draw foldline through center of dart. True stitching lines so dart is symmetrical.

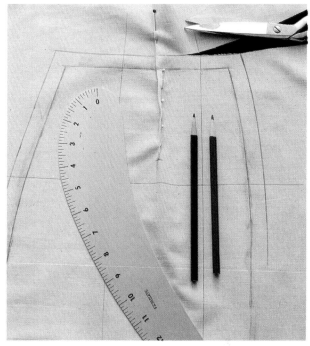

6) True seamlines. Add seam allowances, and trim muslin on cutting lines, with dart pinned in place.

How to Copy Gathers or Ease on a Garment

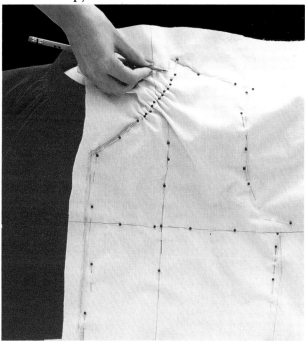

1) Mark and match grainlines of garment and muslin. Smooth and pin muslin up to gathered area. Over a tailor's ham, form gathers or ease in muslin to match fullness in garment. Pin; rub off. Mark area to be gathered or eased.

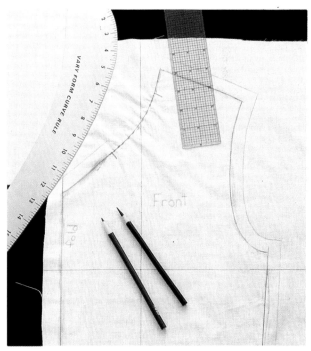

2) True seamlines; add seam allowances and notches to indicate area to be gathered.

Changing Design Details

Some details seen on ready-to-wear garments are easy to copy. Design details can be added to a basic pattern to vary the look. Two details that can be added easily to basic garments are tucks and mock front bands.

Tucks

An easy way to make a garment with tucks is to stitch the tucks in the fabric before cutting out the pattern. Plan the placement of the tucks on the pattern piece. The depth and spacing of the tucks may be varied, but tucks that are ½" (1.3 cm) deep and spaced ½" (1.3 cm) apart work well for many styles. You can add tucks to an entire garment section, or place just a few tucks on the garment.

Cut a piece of fabric for each garment section, allowing enough fabric to stitch the tucks. Because tucks require

extra fabric, yardage requirements for the garment may change.

Always stitch tucks on-grain for smooth stitching and pressing. For diagonal tucks, stitch the tucks on-grain, and place the grainline of the pattern piece on the bias to cut out the fabric (page 91).

It is not necessary to mark all the stitching lines in order to sew tucks. It is easier and more accurate to mark the foldlines only and stitch the depth of the tucks, using a guide on the sewing machine instead of following a marked stitching line.

Mock Front Bands

A mock front band gives the look of a front band on a blouse or dress, but is easier than cutting and applying a separate piece. The method on page 51 adds self-fabric interfacing, facing, and front band, enclosing the raw edge.

Select a pattern with a collar that extends to the front edge of the garment, or beyond it. The upper edge of the band can then be finished by slipstitching the collar over the band.

The mock front band is added to the buttonhole side of the garment; this is the right side on women's garments and the left side on men's. Eliminate the facing pattern piece, or trim off the cut-on facing on the facing foldline.

To determine the width of the mock front band, measure the pattern piece from the center front line to the facing foldline, or to the front seamline; the width of the band will be twice this measurement.

How to Add Tucks

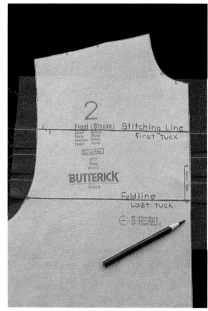

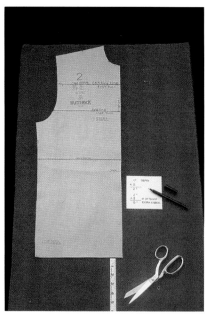

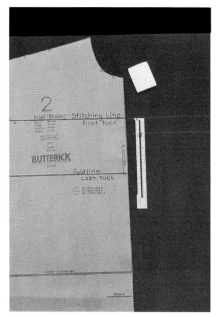

1) Plan desired tucks, determining number, depth, and spacing of tucks. Make test sample. Mark approximate stitching line of first tuck and the approximate foldline of last tuck on pattern piece.

2) Determine amount of extra fabric needed to stitch tucks by multiplying two times the depth of each tuck times the number of tucks. Cut piece of fabric large enough for garment section, allowing extra for tucks.

3) Measure from edge of pattern piece to stitching line of first tuck; mark stitching line on fabric this distance from edge of fabric, using chalk. Mark foldline for first tuck, the depth of tuck away from marked stitching line.

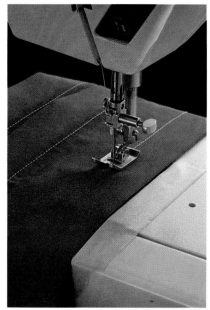

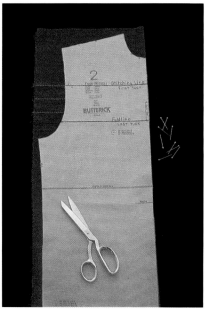

4) Snip-mark stitching lines, and mark remaining foldlines; space between foldlines is two times the depth of tuck plus spacing between stitching lines. Press each foldline, using tip of iron and keeping previously pressed foldlines on top.

5) Mark stitching guide, the depth of tuck from needle, on bed of sewing machine. Stitch tucks, using short stitch length, with foldline on stitching guide.

6) Press tucks in desired direction. Place pattern piece on tucked fabric, matching marked lines; cut fabric. Construct garment following the pattern directions.

How to Add a Mock Front Band

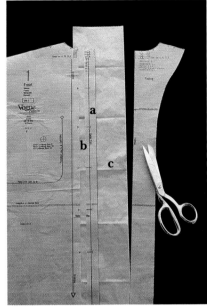

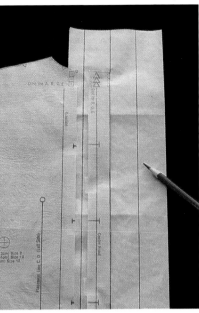

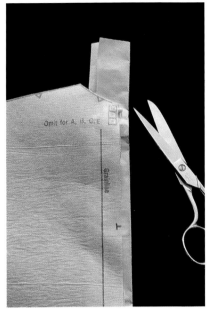

1) Cut pattern on facing foldline; discard facing pattern. Determine width of band (page 49). Slash pattern the width of band minus ¼" (6 mm) from facing foldline or front seamline (**a**). Tape tissue under pattern; spread pattern ½" (1.3 cm) at slash (**b**). Add tissue beyond facing foldline or front seamline, two times width of band (**c**).

2) Mark foldline the width of band away from front edge; mark second foldline on original facing foldline or front seamline of pattern piece. Mark third foldline for tuck through center of tissue at slash.

3) Fold pattern on foldlines, pinning out tuck; trim the tissue to match neck edge.

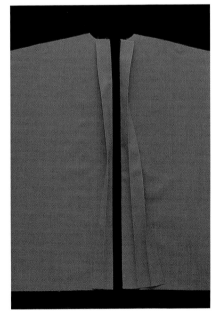

4) Change horizontal buttonhole markings to vertical. Cut buttonhole side of garment from new pattern. Fold out tuck; turn pattern over, and cut button side of garment. Mark foldlines on both pieces.

5) Fold and press buttonhole side of garment, wrong sides together, at the first foldline; fold and press again on second and third foldlines. Fold and press the button side of garment, wrong sides together, on both foldlines.

6) Stitch tuck on buttonhole side of garment, through all layers, ¼" (6 mm) from third foldline, with band facing up. On both front sections, stitch ¼" (6 mm) from front edge through all layers.

Trade Secrets

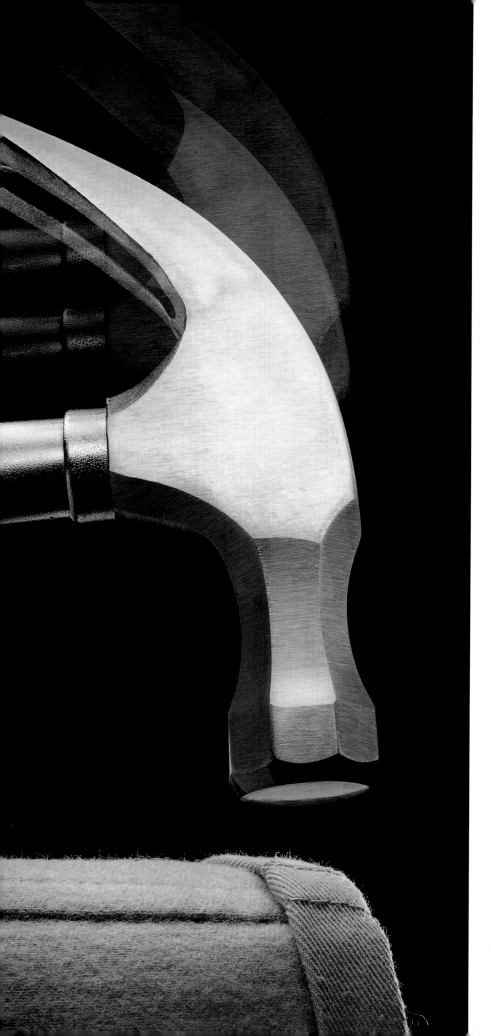

Topstitching Tips

Topstitching is often the focal point of a finished garment. Single or multiple rows of topstitching can add a professional look or accent a special design.

Use paper as a guide for a straight topstitching line. A thin application of spray adhesive or rubber cement on the paper increases friction between the fabric and the paper.

It is sometimes difficult to topstitch around corners on collars, cuffs, or waistbands. A thread tail helps you feed the corner smoothly through the machine.

A fabric or cardboard shim levels the presser foot as you begin topstitching at the edge of fabric or stitch over thick crossing seams. Use one or more layers of fabric or cardboard for desired thickness.

If topstitching thread is not available in the desired color, thread the topstitching needle with two matching or blending strands of all-purpose thread. Tension settings may need to be adjusted when topstitching.

Practice on the same fabric, number of layers, and interfacing that you will use in the garment. Always start with a full bobbin to avoid running out of thread while topstitching.

Flatten thick seams. Use a hammer to pound the seam allowances flat before topstitching on thick or heavy fabrics.

How to Use Paper for Straight Topstitching

1) Apply a thin coating of spray adhesive or rubber cement to one side of paper; allow to dry. Place treated side down on fabric.

2) Align edge of paper to desired topstitching line. Stitch, with paper under presser foot and needle following edge of paper.

How to Use a Thread Tail for Topstitching Corners

1) Take one stitch through corner of fabric, by hand or by machine, leaving long thread tails in fabric.

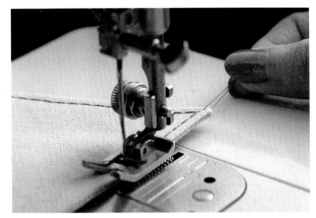

2) Topstitch to corner. Raise presser foot, leaving needle in fabric; pivot. Lower presser foot, and hold onto thread tails as you continue to stitch.

How to Use a Shim for Topstitching

Starting a seam. Place shim under back of presser foot to level it. Start topstitching at edge of fabric.

Crossing a thick seam. 1) Stitch until you approach thick seam and front of presser foot starts to lift. Place the shim behind presser foot to level it.

2) Stitch onto thick seam until presser foot starts to tip down; place shim in front of seam to level presser foot. Stitch until presser foot is completely on shim. Remove shim, and continue stitching.

Easy Flat-fell Seams

Flat-fell seams are often seen in sportswear, but they can also be used in other types of clothing. They are used for decorative purposes as well as for durability.

The easy method shown here eliminates the trimming necessary in the traditional flat-fell seam, yet the results are essentially the same. It is important to use the entire ⅝" (1.5 cm) seam allowance so the finished garment is the right size and so adjoining sections will match.

How to Sew a Flat-fell Seam without Trimming

1) Fold ⅜" (1 cm) seam allowance to wrong side on one garment section; press. Position the corresponding garment section with raw edge on foldline, so sections are wrong sides together.

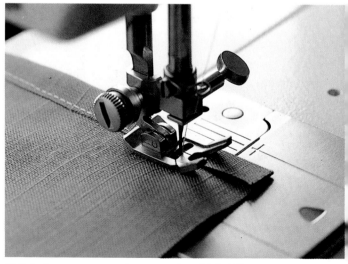

2) Stitch garment sections together ⁵⁄₁₆" (7.5 mm) from foldline.

3) Lay garment flat, right side up. Fold and press seam allowance so raw edge is enclosed.

4) Stitch along foldline through all layers; space rows of stitching 5/16" (7.5 mm) apart.

Simple Tab Plackets

A tab placket is usually seen on the cuffs of men's ready-to-wear shirts. Long-sleeved blouses and lightweight jackets can also be constructed with tab plackets. Or this type of placket can be used at the front neckline of a pullover shirt.

The tab placket is made from a rectangular strip of fabric and can be sewn without a pattern. Careful measuring and pressing are essential for this easy timesaving method.

How to Sew a Simple Tab Placket

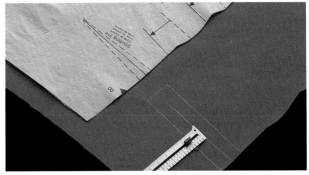

1) Mark placket position on garment, using pattern. Mark stitching lines ½" (1.3 cm) on each side of placket line and ½" (1.3 cm) above placket line.

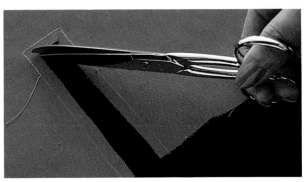

2) Staystitch end of box around corners. Trim away center of box, leaving ¼" (6 mm) seam allowances. Clip to corners.

3) Cut fabric strip on straight grain, 2½" (6.5 cm) wide and the length of stitching line plus 1" (2.5 cm).

4) Press fabric strip in half lengthwise, *wrong* sides together. Press under ¼" (6 mm) on one long edge of strip. Press under slightly less than ¼" (6 mm) on the remaining long edge.

5) Place folded edges of strip around edges of placket, with narrow side of strip lapped slightly over the staystitching line on right side of fabric. Edgestitch through all layers, pulling strip into straight line.

6) Fold overlap at right angle to underlap. Press strip only, to form a point. Fold overlap over underlap, forming a point at the top; press. Edgestitch around point, 1" (2.5 cm) down sides and across placket, to form box. Trim ends of strip. Apply cuff.

Quick Shirring

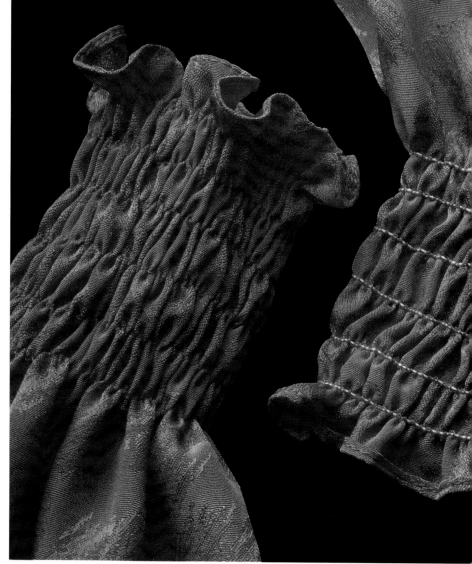

Several rows of shirred elastic are attractive and comfortable on a lightweight garment. Shirr the cuffs, waistline, bodice, or skirt yoke for a decorative look.

Elastic threads, held in place with zigzag stitching on the wrong side of the fabric and adjusted to desired fullness, can be used as a part of the garment design.

How to Shirr with Elastic Thread

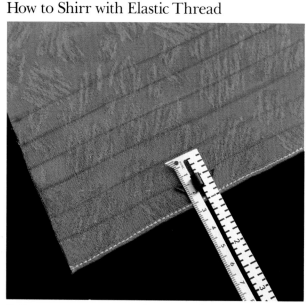

1) Leave one seam open in area to be shirred. Mark rows for shirring on the wrong side of fabric, using chalk or water-soluble marking pen. Space rows ½" to ¾" (1.3 to 2 cm) apart.

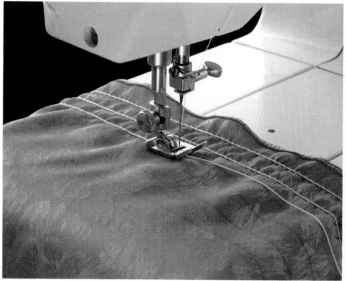

2) Place elastic thread over marked lines. Set the machine for a zigzag stitch just wide enough to sew over elastic. Without stretching elastic or catching it in stitching, zigzag over elastic on all marked lines. Leave long tails of elastic on both ends.

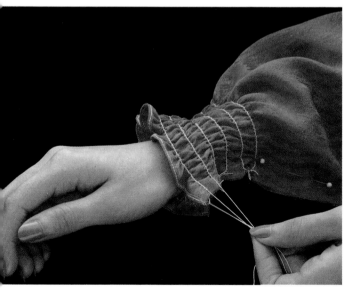

3) Pin seamline, and try on garment, wrong side out. Pull elastic tails two rows at a time to keep the shirring even. Tie knots at ends of rows; cut off tails.

4) Stitch the seam, using short, straight stitches, pulling elastic thread knots out of the way of the presser foot. Reinforce by stitching again over the elastic threads. Finish seam allowances.

Comfortable Waistbands

You can sew a comfortable waistband for pants or a skirt by substituting nonroll elastic for interfacing. This does not make the waistband stretchy, but provides wearing comfort, because it snugs up the ease. The nonroll elastic prevents the waistband from folding over, so it is always neat and comfortable.

Ease is necessary for the success of this method. Do not eliminate the ease built into the pattern; you may want to add ½" to 1" (1.3 to 2.5 cm) more ease for added comfort.

Use elastic that is equal to the finished width of the waistband and slightly shorter than the length of the finished waistband. The elastic is anchored at the ends by the closures.

How to Make a Waistband with Nonroll Elastic

1) Trim ¼" (6 mm) from one long edge of waistband, and zigzag edge to finish; or overlock one long edge, trimming ¼" (6 mm) with knives. Stitch waistband to garment, raw edges even and right sides together. Grade seam allowances, and press toward waistband.

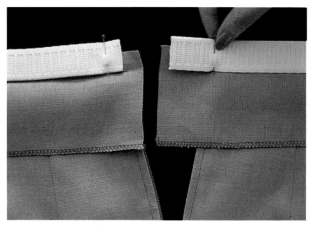

2) Cut elastic ½" to 1" (1.3 to 2.5 cm) shorter than finished waistband measurement. Place edge of elastic on wrong side of fabric, over waistband seam allowance next to stitching. Match ends of elastic to seamlines at ends of waistband; pin ends.

3) Pin elastic to seam allowances, stretching slightly to fit waistband. Zigzag along lower edge of elastic through elastic and seam allowances.

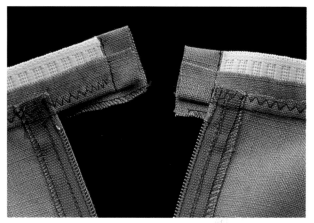

4) Press seam allowances toward waistband. Fold waistband, right sides together, even with upper edge of elastic. Stitch ends of waistband; do not catch elastic in stitches. Trim corners, and grade seam allowances.

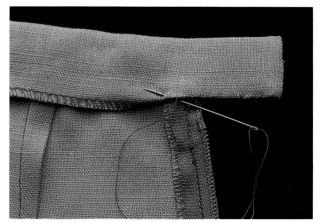

5) Turn waistband right side out, enclosing elastic; press. Fold seam allowance inside the underlap of waistband; slipstitch.

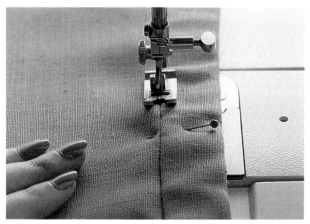

6) Stitch in the ditch from right side of garment, catching extended seam allowance on inside of waistband. Attach heavy-duty hook and eye, securing ends of elastic in stitching.

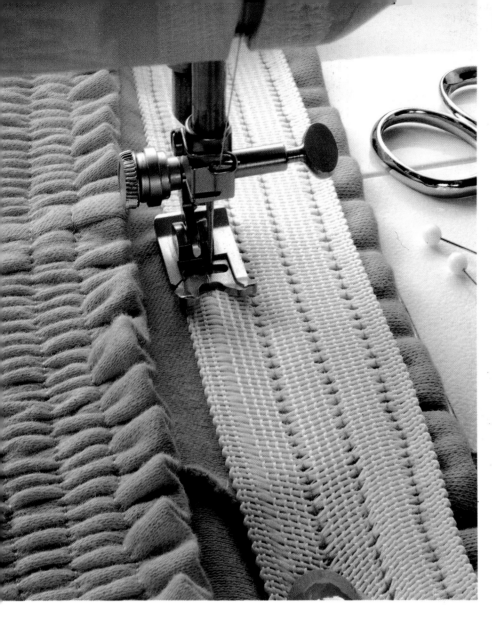

Sport Elastic

Achieve the look of ready-to-wear with multiple rows of stitching in elasticized waistbands of skirts or pants. The same sport elastic used by ready-to-wear manufacturers is available for home sewers.

Sport elastic is applied by stitching through several nonelasticized rows. This prevents piercing elasticized threads with the needle, which weakens the elastic. The rows in the elastic also provide a guide for easy straight stitching.

Sport elastic, softer and lighter in weight than most elastics, is especially comfortable and suitable for use in sportswear. Because it may stretch out more than regular elastic when applied, you may want to make a trial waistband from the garment fabric to check the stretch and recovery of the elastic. Make a note of the length of elastic you started with, for future reference.

How to Apply Sport Elastic

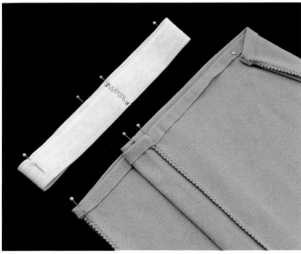

1) Cut elastic 3" to 5" (7.5 to 12.5 cm) shorter than waist measurement. Overlap ends, and zigzag together. On upper edge of garment, fold ½" (1.3 cm) to wrong side. Divide the elastic and garment waistline into fourths; pin-mark.

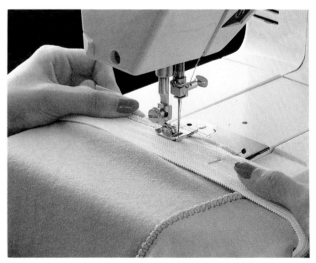

2) Place elastic on wrong side of garment ¼" (6 mm) below fold, matching marks; pin. Stretch, and stitch in the nonelasticized rows, using 8 to 10 stitches per inch (2.5 cm).

Transparent Elastic

Transparent elastic is made from 100% polyurethane that stretches to three times its original length. It is a soft, lightweight elastic with an opaque appearance, and is suitable for lightweight to mediumweight fabrics. It may be used for elasticized swimwear openings, because it is chlorine-resistant. Or use it as a stabilizer for heavy knits by stitching it into the seams to prevent them from stretching out of shape, while providing give.

Do not reuse transparent elastic once it has been stitched; too many needle holes will weaken it.

How to Apply Transparent Elastic

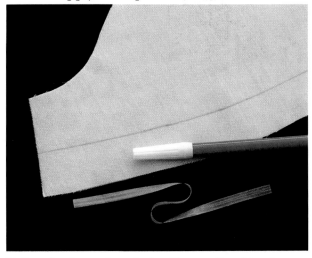

1) Cut elastic to a length that fits comfortably plus overlap. Mark stitching line on wrong side of garment.

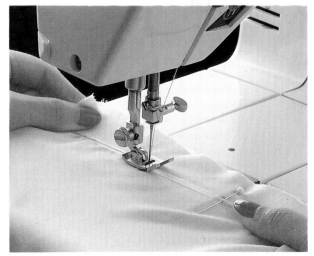

2) Divide garment and elastic into fourths; mark. Match marks, and stitch elastic to garment on conventional machine, using long straight or zigzag stitches; stretch elastic to fit.

Smooth-fitting Zipper in Stretch Fabric

This exposed zipper application is used for close-fitting garments made from two-way stretch knits. Zippers are frequently used in ski racing suits or skating dresses that have high, fitted necklines. When this method is used, the garment does not bind or pucker in the zipper area, because it is stretched to fit before the zipper is applied.

For this method, a pattern that has either ¼" (6 mm) or ⅝" (1.5 cm) seam allowances for the zipper opening may be used.

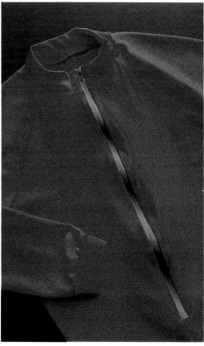

Garment ripples in the zipper area when off the body, but is smooth-fitting when it is worn.

How to Sew a Zipper in Two-way Stretch Knit

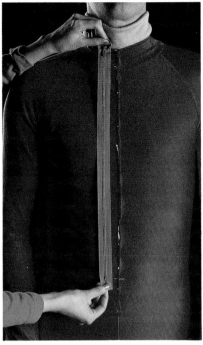

1) Try on garment, pinning zipper opening closed. Place zipper at seam; mark placement of top and bottom zipper stops on garment.

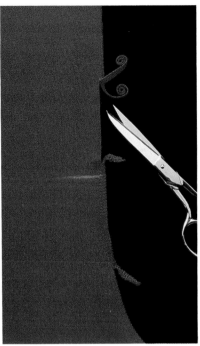

2) Remove garment and adjust the stitching of the crotch seam to ¼" (6 mm) above bottom mark. Trim off seam allowances of the zipper opening.

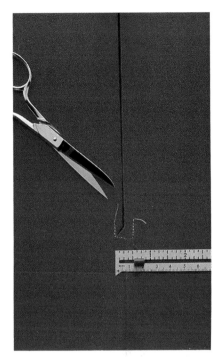

3) Mark ½" (1.3 cm) across bottom zipper placement mark and ¼" (6 mm) from edges of opening; stitch. Clip diagonally into corners, but not through stitching.

4) Divide zipper into fourths; mark. Divide zipper opening into fourths; mark.

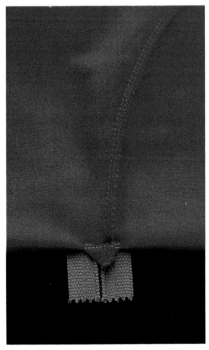

5) Fold lower part of garment up, exposing clipped triangle. Place zipper under garment, right side up, so stitching is just below zipper stop. Stitch twice across triangle just above stitching to secure zipper.

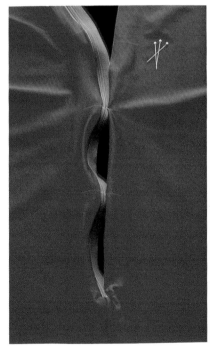

6) Pin zipper tape to one edge of zipper opening, matching marks, with right sides together and edges even. Stitch ¼" (6 mm) seam, stretching fabric between marks. Repeat for other edge of zipper opening. Complete garment.

Lapped Zipper & Facing

Zippers are a frequently used closure for garments. This zipper application uses machine stitching instead of hand sewing to attach the facings neatly and without bulk.

Lapped zippers should always be used at side seams, but may also be used for center back openings.

In the steps that follow, right or left side refers to the right or left side as the garment is to be worn.

How to Sew a Lapped Zipper and Facing

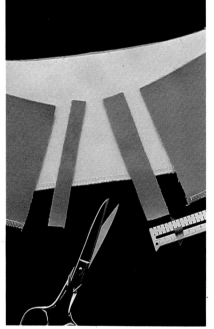

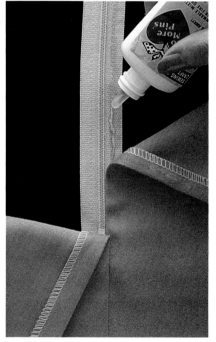

1) Trim ½" (1.3 cm) from edge of right facing at zipper opening; trim ¾" (2 cm) from edge of left facing. Apply interfacing; stitch facing seams, and finish lower edge.

2) Measure zipper, from bottom stop to top stop, plus 1" (2.5 cm); mark position for bottom stop on seam allowance. Stitch seam up to mark. Press right seam allowance under ½" (1.3 cm); press left seam allowance under ⅝" (1.5 cm).

3) Glue-baste right seam allowance to closed zipper, positioning bottom stop at mark, and fold close to zipper teeth; work from the right side of the garment.

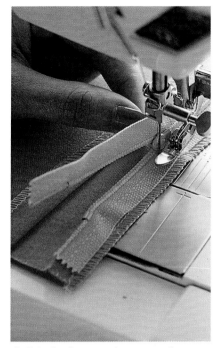

4) Stitch close to zipper teeth through extended right seam allowance, using zipper foot. As you approach top of zipper, open zipper partway, raising and lowering presser foot. Continue stitching.

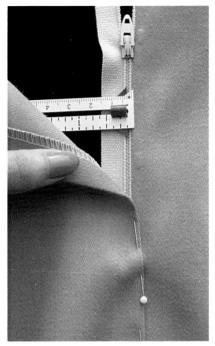

5) Close zipper. Lap left side of garment scant ⅛" (3 mm) over right side; pin-baste.

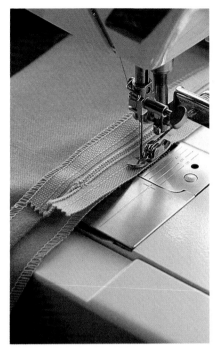

6) Baste through center of zipper tape and extended seam allowance, basting from the top of zipper to the bottom. Zipper tape extends slightly beyond seam allowance.

7) Open zipper. With right sides together and raw edges even, join ends of facing and seam allowances of zipper seam in ¼" (6 mm) seam.

8) Match and pin seams of garment and facing, right sides together and raw edges even. Zipper tape will lie flat, and zipper teeth will be toward fold. On underlap side, zipper teeth fit tightly against fold. Stitch facing to garment.

9) Grade the seam allowances. Turn right side out, and press. Understitch as close to zipper as possible. Topstitch overlap. Attach hook and eye.

Centered Zipper & Facing

This easy method for applying a centered zipper uses machine stitching for a neat closure and eliminates the need for hand sewing to attach the facings.

A centered zipper application can be used at a faced neckline of a dress or blouse, or at a faced waistline in skirts or pants.

How to Sew a Centered Zipper and Facing

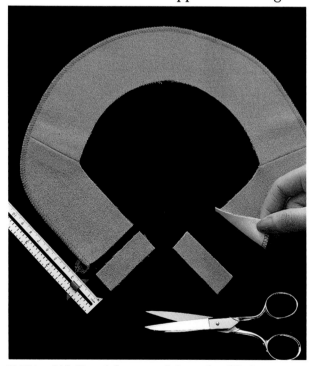

1) Trim ¾" (2 cm) from straight ends of facings; apply interfacing. Stitch facing seams. Finish edge.

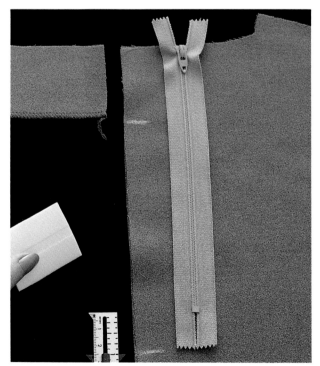

2) Measure length of zipper plus 1" (2.5 cm) for top seam allowance and hook and eye. Mark bottom zipper position and width of facing on seam allowance.

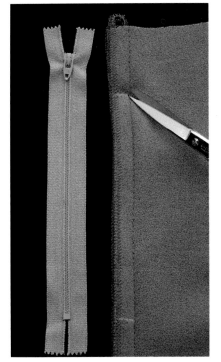

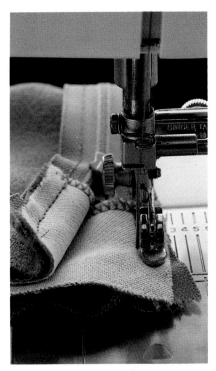

3) Stitch seam to bottom zipper mark. Baste zipper seam. Finish seam allowances. Clip basting at facing mark. Press seam open.

4) Center zipper, face down, on seam allowances, with bottom stop at mark; pin or baste. Machine-baste zipper to seam allowances, pulling zipper tape into seam allowance at top.

5) Remove basting in seam above facing mark. Open zipper, and stitch ends of facing to garment with ¼" (6 mm) seam.

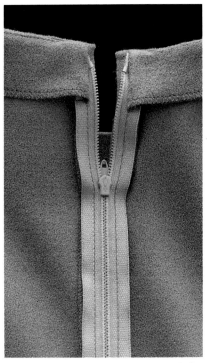

6) Match and pin seams of garment and facing, with right sides together and raw edges even. Fold seam allowances toward facing; pin. Stitch neckline seam.

7) Grade and clip seam. Turn right side out; press. Understitch as close to zipper as possible.

8) Topstitch bottom and one side of zipper; then stitch back across bottom and up other side. Remove basting. Attach hook and eye.

Buttons
& Buttonholes

The choice of buttons is a major consideration on any garment or project. A customized look can be achieved by creating Chinese ball buttons (pages 74 and 75) or chrysanthemum buttons (pages 116 and 117). Covered buttons, opposite, can be made in a variety of sizes and shapes.

To determine placement of buttons and buttonholes on a blouse or bodice front, mark the placement for one buttonhole at the fullest part of the bustline. Space others evenly from that position. Check the guidelines below to determine whether buttonholes should be vertical or horizontal.

Tips for Vertical or Horizontal Buttonhole Placement

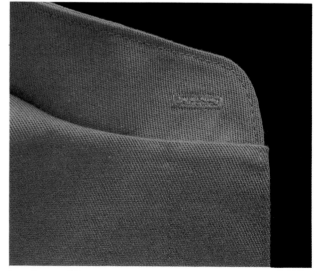

Vertical buttonholes work well with lightweight fabrics and small buttons. They are commonly used for shirt plackets, shirt or blouse front bands, or pocket flaps.

Horizontal buttonholes are used for stability in areas of stress, such as on cuffs, neck bands or waistbands. Buttonholes on jackets and coats are usually horizontal.

Tips for Making Covered Buttons

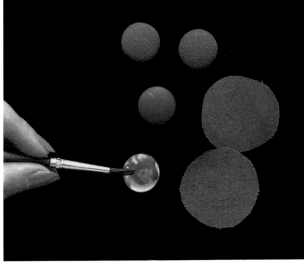

Paint metal button to match fabric color to prevent show-through of metal when using sheer or loosely woven fabric. Or use two layers of sheer fabric.

Wet washable fabric, and stretch it over metal button for a smooth fit when covering a button.

Chinese Ball Buttons

Chinese ball buttons can be used with buttonholes, button loops, or frog closures (pages 76 and 77).

Cord-filled bias tubing is used to make the buttons, because it has body and shapes well. Chinese ball buttons can be made from one or more strands of bias tubing. Select lightweight fabrics for smooth knots.

Two strands of ⅛" (3 mm) cord-filled bias tubing make a ¾" (2 cm) ball button; one strand makes a ½" (1.3 cm) button. To make the tubing, you will need two 24" (61 cm) lengths of ³⁄₃₂" cording and two 1" × 12" (2.5 × 30.5 cm) bias strips of lightweight fabric.

How to Make Cord-filled Bias Tubing

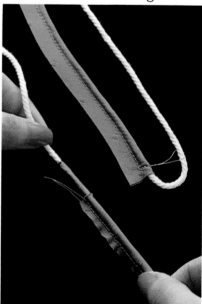

Fold bias strip around cord, right sides together and raw edges even. Using zipper foot, stitch loosely along cord. Stitch across strip and cord at middle of the length of cord; trim seam allowances. Slide strip over exposed cord, turning right side out. Cut off stitched end of fabric and excess cord.

How to Make Chinese Ball Buttons

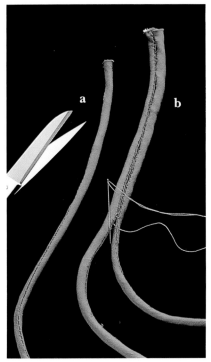

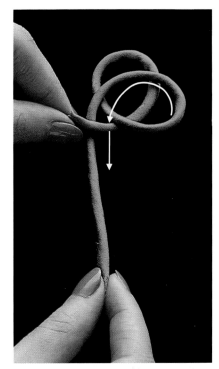

1) Make cord-filled bias tubing, opposite. Use one 12" (30.5 cm) piece **(a)** for each single-strand button. Or use two 12" (30.5 cm) pieces **(b)** for each double-strand button; slipstitch loosely together.

2) Loop the long end of the tubing as shown. (It may be helpful to pin end of tubing to a padded surface.)

3) Loop tubing a second time, over first loop and under tail.

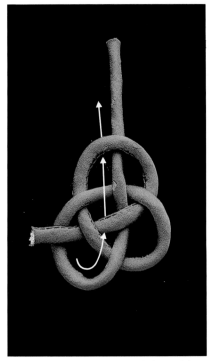

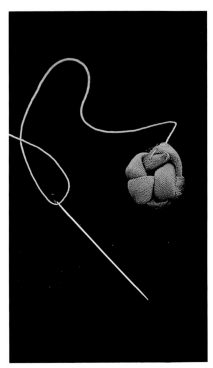

4) Weave the loose end of the tubing over and under previous loops.

5) Pull on both ends of the tubing, gently easing knot into a ball.

6) Cut ends of tubing so they overlap under the button; whipstitch. Make thread shank, covering it with closely spaced blanket stitch.

Frog Closures

Frog closures are often used with Chinese ball buttons for a traditional Oriental appearance. Although there are some ready-made frogs available, the selection is limited, so you may want to make your own.

Frog closures can be made from purchased braid or cord-filled bias tubing to match or contrast with the garment. The cording or braid can be knotted or arranged in many ways for a variety of styles. The

choice of fabric, the diameter of the cording, and the size of the loops add further variety.

To make your own cord-filled bias tubing (page 74), cut a bias strip for each frog about 60" (152.5 cm) long; for a frog with a Chinese ball button, cut a bias strip about 72" (183 cm) long. The length of bias tubing required depends on the diameter of the tubing.

How to Make Frog Closures

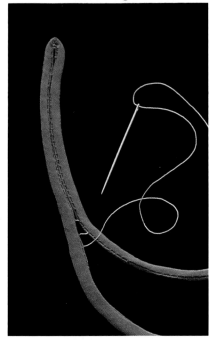

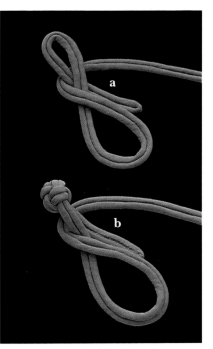

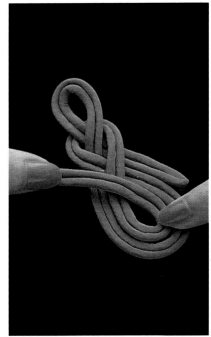

1) Cut bias strips, left. Make cord-filled bias tubing (page 74). Fold tubing in half, and slipstitch strands together from the back. Work with tubing face up when making frogs.

2) Form one end of tubing into a small top loop and a large bottom loop. Bring other end around small loop to back **(a)**. For a frog with a Chinese ball button **(b)**, make button (pages 74 and 75), starting 4" (10 cm) from one end of tubing; position button at top of small loop.

3) Bring long end around to front, and form another loop to fit inside large bottom loop, following the direction of the original loop.

4) Carry long end up and around small top loop, below previous loop; bring end around to front, and form a loop to fit inside other large bottom loops.

5) Carry long end up and around the small top loop, below previous loops; bring end down to center of large bottom loops, and insert in center. Pull through to secure.

6) Adjust small loop to size of ball button. Trim loose ends of tubing; slipstitch ends and loops in place on wrong side.

Button Loops

Button loops are a subtle way of adding interest to a garment. While they are always functional and often the only way of solving closure problems of spacing and overlap, they are also one of the most overlooked ways of adding a fine sewing appearance.

Button loops can be made from all-purpose thread, crochet cotton, or pearl cotton. They are almost unnoticeable when made from matching thread.

How to Make and Attach a Hand-crocheted Button Loop

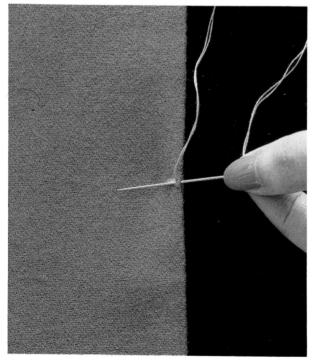

1) **Mark** position of loop on garment. Using two strands of knotted thread, insert needle and thread through mark from inside the garment. Take a small stitch, leaving a 4" (10 cm) loop.

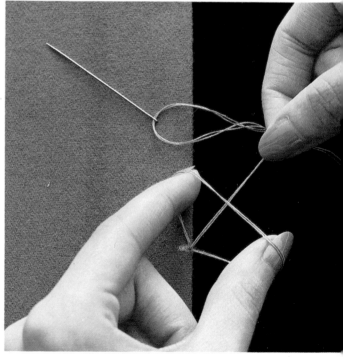

2) **Hold** loop open with thumb and index finger of left hand; hold thread taut with index finger and thumb of right hand.

How to Make a Machine-sewn Button Loop

1) Zigzag over several strands of thread, using a conventional sewing machine; hold thread taut, and pull gently through machine. Or make tail chain on the overlock, using the rolled hem setting.

2) Thread tapestry needle with button looping. Insert needle through garment from wrong side and then back through garment, the desired distance from stitch, leaving tails on the wrong side; tie together in a knot.

3) Pull thread through loop and pull taut, close to fabric; new loop will be formed. Repeat steps 2 and 3 until button loop is desired length.

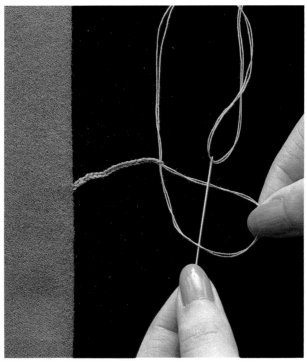

4) Pull needle and thread through the last loop to tighten and secure chain. Insert needle in garment desired distance from first stitch; draw thread through, and tie knot.

Using Fasteners in New Ways

Metal shanks on buttons can sometimes wear through the threads that hold them to the garment. To prevent this, the button can be sewn on by linking an eye portion of a hook and eye through the shank of the button and then stitching the eye to the garment. Use a straight eye to keep the shank the same length, or use a round eye to extend the shank for heavy coats.

For a closure in an area where garment edges meet, rather than overlap, you can attach a hanging snap instead of a hook and eye or button and loop closure. One half of the snap is applied in the usual manner; the other half is attached at the edge of the garment by two of the four holes, with the rest of the snap hanging free.

Two New Ways to Use Fasteners

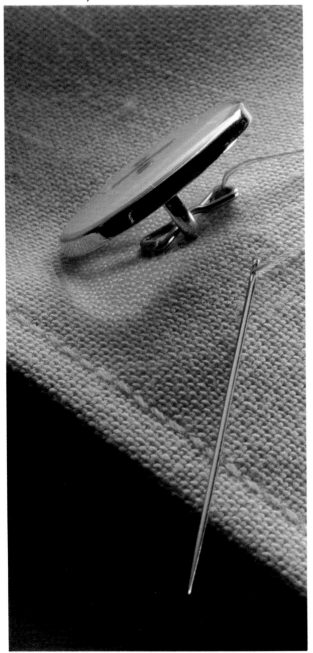

Metal-shank buttons. Link the eye portion of a hook and eye through the shank; stitch eye to garment.

Hanging snap. Stitch ball half of snap to facing on one side of garment. Attach socket half to other side, stitching several times through two holes.

Reinforcing Slits & Skirt Front Closures

Slits and buttonholes at lower edge of straight skirts can tear unless the garment is reinforced. For skirts with slits, stitch a straight eye portion of a hook and eye to the wrong side of the garment at the top of a slit to prevent the seam from ripping. When the garment is strained, the metal eye takes the stress.

To reinforce the lower button closure on a front-opening skirt, machine-stitch around the bottom buttonhole through both sides of skirt front, and attach button through all layers. The buttonhole is nonfunctioning, but the garment will not tear if subjected to stress.

Two New Ways to Add Reinforcement

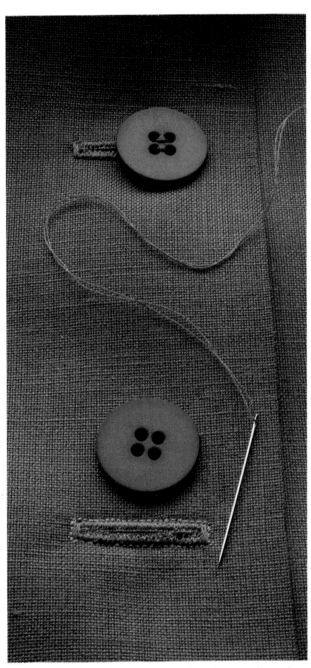

Reinforcing a slit. Stitch straight eye portion of hook and eye to wrong side of garment at top of skirt slit. Stitching should not be visible on right side of garment.

Reinforcing lower buttonhole. Align closure, fastening all but lower button. Using small stitches, straight-stitch around outer edge of buttonhole through all layers. Attach button.

Designer Techniques

Circular Ruffles with a Flair

Circular ruffles get their name from the ring-shaped circles of fabric used to make them. Because of the way they are cut and sewn, without seamline gathers, they do not add bulk at the seamline.

Commercial patterns that have this design feature include a pattern piece for the ruffle, but you can make your own pattern if you want to add a circular ruffle to another garment. Draw the circles to any dimension; a smaller inner circle makes fuller ruffles, while a larger inner circle makes ruffles that are less full. The depth of the ruffle, the distance between the inner and outer circles, can also be adjusted to give a variety of effects. You may want to cut a test piece from fabric and open it out to check the fullness.

To determine the number of circular pieces to cut for the ruffle, measure the distance around the inner seamline of the pattern and subtract ½" (1.3 cm) for seam allowances. Divide that measurement into the length of the area to which the ruffle will be applied.

One way to finish circular ruffles is to line them, using self-fabric or a fabric that is lighter in weight or contrasting in color. The lining completely encloses the raw edges and gives a smooth finish. Or finish unlined circular ruffles with French seams and hem them, using the method for a machine-stitched narrow hem, pages 104 and 105, or the rolled hem on an overlock machine.

How to Make a Pattern for a Circular Ruffle

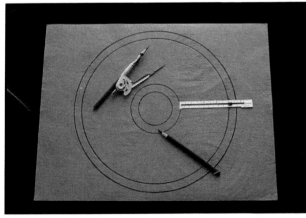

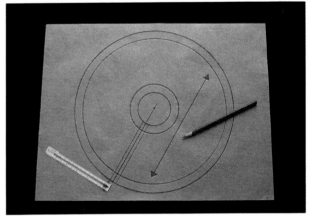

1) Draw pattern on paper, starting with a 4" (10 cm) circle, or the desired measurement. Draw another circle 4" (10 cm) larger, or the desired amount of ruffle depth. Add ⅝" (1.5 cm) seam allowances to outer and inner edges of circle.

2) Mark opening from edge to center of circle. Mark ¼" (6 mm) seamlines on each side of opening. Mark grainline parallel to opening.

How to Make a Lined Circular Ruffle

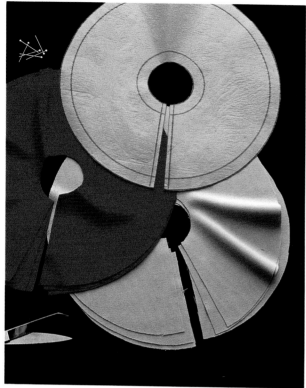

1) Cut ruffle pieces from garment fabric and lining, using pattern; to determine number of pieces to cut, see page 84.

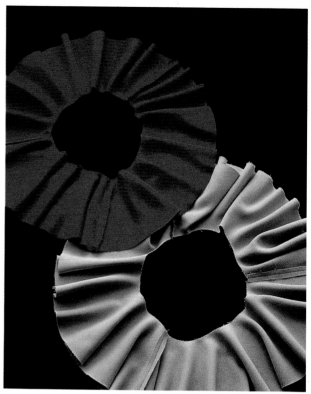

2) Stitch pieces cut from garment fabric, right sides together on straight edges, using ¼" (6 mm) seams; repeat for lining pieces. Press seams open.

3) Stitch lining and ruffle, right sides together, on outer circle seamline. Press seam flat to embed stitches.

4) Press seam open over tailor's ham or curved tailor's board.

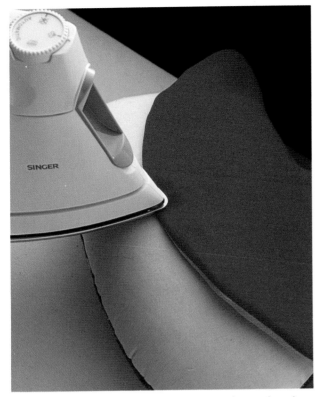

5) Turn right side out, and press outer edge, using tip of iron. Trim seam allowance to ⅛" (3 mm).

6) Stitch both layers, wrong sides together, at inner edge just inside seamline.

7) Clip seam allowances to stitching at regular intervals of ½" to 2" (1.3 to 5 cm), depending on tightness of curve.

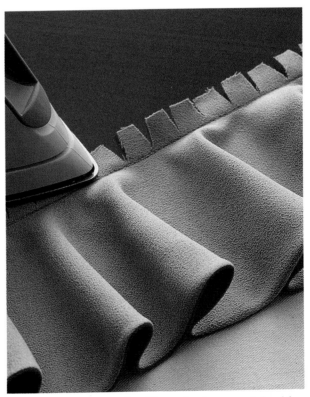

8) Match seamlines of ruffle and garment, right sides together; stitch. Lightly press seam allowance away from ruffle.

Soft Bias Ruffles

Because bias resists wrinkles, bias ruffles are soft and stay full with few creases. Bias ruffles can be gathered more fully than ruffles cut on either the lengthwise or the crosswise grain of the same fabric, because fabric narrows as it is pulled along the bias. The bias edge does not have to be finished, because it will not ravel.

To make bias ruffles, use a double width of self-fabric, folded in half lengthwise. Bias ruffles should be gathered with three or four rows of gathering stitches to keep the seam flat while the ruffle is attached to the garment.

For a bias ruffle that has more body, interface it with bias-cut organza.

Use a straightedge and a chalk wheel marker for accurate cutting lines. For a tightly gathered ruffle, cut the bias strips 3 to 4 times the finished length and 2 times the finished width plus 1¼" (3.2 cm) for seam allowances. For a ruffle with less fullness, cut the strips 1½ to 2½ times the finished length.

How to Make Bias Ruffles

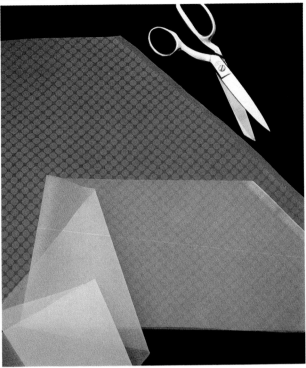

1) Cut bias strips for ruffle, opposite. For ruffles that have more body, cut bias strip of organza interfacing half the cut width of ruffle.

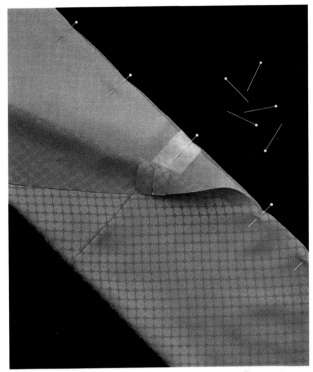

2) Seam ruffle strips together; seam organza strips. Place organza on wrong side of ruffle, even with one raw edge. On flat surface, fold the ruffle in half, wrong sides together. To maintain a soft look, do not crease folded edge. Align the three layers at raw edges; pin.

3) Stitch three rows of gathering stitches through all layers, with first row on seamline. Pull all rows at the same time, and adjust gathers evenly. Knot gathering threads after adjusting.

4) Place ruffle on garment, with right sides together and raw edges even; stitch. Stitch again ⅛" (3 mm) inside seamline. Grade seam allowances. Do not remove remaining gathering threads.

Bias-cut Garments

Bias-cut garments are comfortable to wear, and they drape softly. A bias-cut garment follows body curves more closely than a garment cut on the straight grain.

Bias-cut garments are cut on true bias, a 45-degree angle between the lengthwise and crosswise grainlines of fabric. Cut 1½" (3.8 cm) seam allowances on bias straight seams, because the fibers near the cut edge spread, making the cut edge longer than its original length.

Tips for Sewing Bias-cut Garments

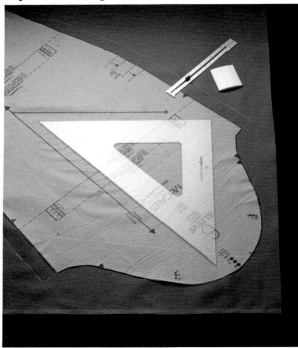

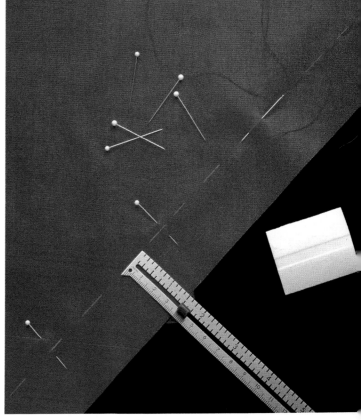

Mark new grainline on pattern at 45-degree angle to original grainline. Place pattern on single layer of fabric, with new grainline on lengthwise grain of fabric. Cut out, with 1½" (3.8 cm) seam allowances on straight seams. Turn over to cut second piece.

Mark seamline with chalk to ensure accurate stitching. Hand-baste seams, with fabric layers on flat surface to prevent distortion. Break basting thread about every 10" (25.5 cm) on long seams, so bias is not restricted. Leave unknotted tails at end of each thread.

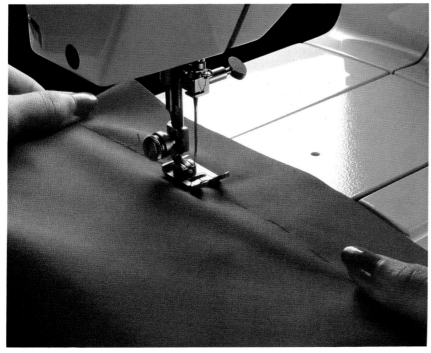

Stretch fabric slightly as you stitch bias seams, to provide the required give in the seams and to prevent puckering.

Hang bias garments for at least 24 hours before hemming, because bias seams tend to stretch. Pin waistline of skirt to hanger, placing pins 1" (2.5 cm) apart. Hang blouse or bodice on padded hanger, with shoulder pads in place.

Shaping Garments with Boning

Boning is the secret to a smooth fit in close-fitting evening wear and some swimsuits. Although the name "boning" has not changed since corsets were made from whalebone, the product itself has. Today's product is either a plastic strip covered with woven fabric or nonwoven interfacing, or it is made from heavy polypropylene filaments interwoven with polyester.

Garments shaped with boning need to be closely fitted with little or no ease allowance. Even full-busted women use boning in strapless garments to prevent the bodice from shifting while wearing.

Strips of boning can be applied to lined or unlined garments in any area requiring support. Boning is usually applied to vertical seams. On unlined garments it is sewn to the seam allowances. On lined garments it can be sewn to the inside of the lining on a placement line so it is completely hidden.

Boning has a built-in curve which contours smoothly. Position it so the ends curve toward the body of the wearer. When the closely fitted garment is worn, it will fit smoothly.

How to Attach Plastic Boning

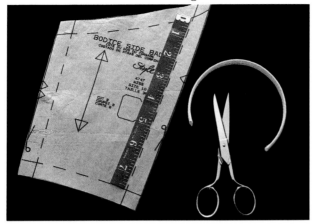

1) Cut boning 1" (2.5 cm) longer than placement line where boning will be applied.

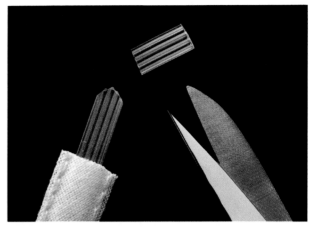

2) Push boning strip out of the end of the covering. Trim away ½" (1.3 cm) of the boning, rounding off any sharp corners. Repeat for other end.

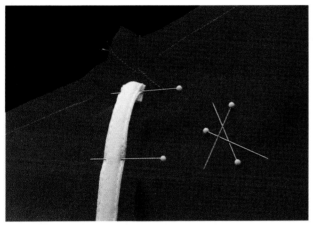

3) Fold ends of covering over boning to the wrong side. Place boning over seam or marked lines, with ends curving toward the body.

4) Machine-stitch edges of covering to garment seam allowances or to lining, using general-purpose presser foot.

How to Attach Polypropylene Boning

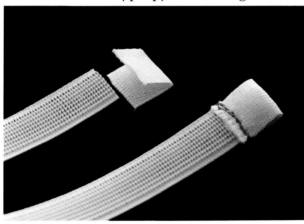

1) Cut boning to length of placement line where boning will be applied. Cut a 1" (2.5 cm) piece of ½" (1.3 cm) twill tape for each end. Fold in half, and place over end of boning. Stitch through all layers about ⅜" (1 cm) from end of boning.

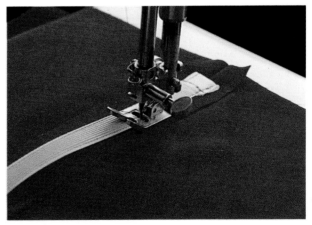

2) Place boning in position, with ends curving toward the body. Machine-stitch edges of boning to garment seam allowances or to lining, using general-purpose presser foot.

The Mystery of Single-thread Sewing

To eliminate knotted threads or backstitching, which can detract from the appearance of tucks or darts in sheer fabrics, use single-thread sewing.

Single-thread sewing can be done on any sewing machine, using the threading technique, below. This threading process is repeated for each tuck or dart.

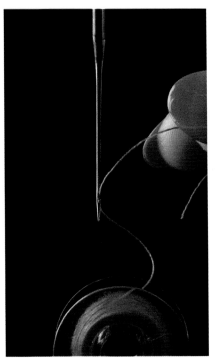

Thread sewing machine, using only the bobbin thread. The bobbin thread is threaded backward through the needle, thread guides, and tension discs.

How to Sew Single-thread Tucks and Darts

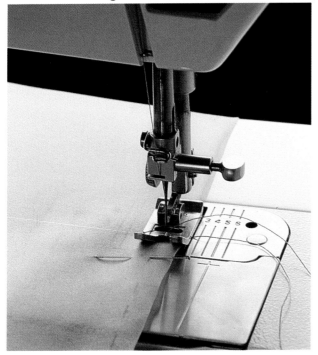

Tucks. 1) Mark stitching lines for tucks, using water-soluble marking pen or chalk. Fold fabric, *wrong* sides together, matching marked lines. With machine threaded normally, lower needle into fabric at lower end of tuck.

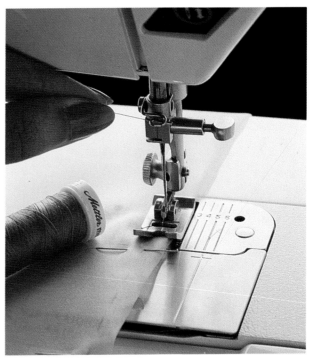

2) Pull bobbin thread up through fabric layers; remove spool of thread from machine. Thread bobbin thread backward through the needle, thread guides, and tension discs. Pull thread beyond tension discs, to a length longer than finished tuck, so machine tension will control it.

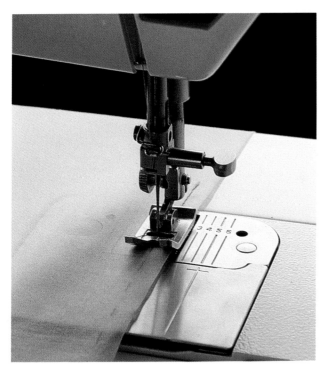

3) Stitch tuck; press. Repeat threading and stitching process for each tuck.

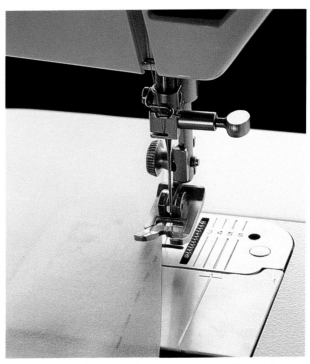

Darts. Pull up bobbin thread, and thread machine as in step 2, above. Stitch dart, beginning at point; press.

Designing with Striped Fabric

Pleat out and stitch through some of the stripes to eliminate them and to create a coordinating fabric for part of a garment. Depending on which stripes are eliminated, different effects can be achieved with the same fabric. For another effect, tucks can be sewn in striped fabric, using the stripes as stitching lines (pages 98 and 99).

A striped fabric can also be cut into strips across the stripes and sewn together for a patchwork design.

Before purchasing the yardage for sewing the garment, you may want to experiment with a small piece of fabric to plan the desired effect and to help determine the amount of fabric needed. These techniques are recommended for woven fabrics only.

Creating Coordinating Striped Fabrics

Pleat out and stitch through some of the stripes in a striped fabric to create a coordinating striped fabric that can be used for collars, cuffs, and other details.

Place the pattern piece on the new fabric, and cut out the garment section. Finish the raw edges or underline the garment to prevent the seams from raveling.

Conceal some of the colors in a striped fabric, piecing the fabric so only two or three colors are featured.

Create tucked fabric by stitching along selected stripes, wrong sides together.

How to Make Coordinating Striped Fabrics

1) Fold fabric, right sides together, aligning edge of stripes (arrow). Pin or baste.

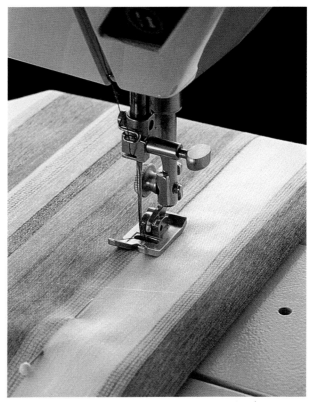

2) Stitch slightly deeper than edge of stripes to ensure that color is hidden.

3) Slash fold, or trim seam allowances to ¼" (6 mm). Press seam open. Repeat until fabric is the desired length or width.

Tucked fabric. Fold fabric, *wrong* sides together, and stitch on edge of stripe. Press tucks to one side.

Creating Patchwork Fabrics

Cut a striped fabric apart and stitch it together in a new way to create a coordinating fabric. Creating a new design requires planning, careful fabric and pattern selection, and accurate sewing.

A variety of effects can be achieved, depending on the width of the stripe, the number of colors, and whether the fabric has even or uneven stripes. The design can also be changed by varying the width of the cut strips. This pieced fabric works best as a border on a shirt or top, or for small areas of a blouse or dress, such as pockets, yokes, or cuffs.

Create a fabric with a new look by stitching strips of striped fabric together in a staggered pattern.

Stitch strips of striped fabric together to create a checkerboard effect. Vary the width of the cut strips, or cut all strips the same width.

Add soutache braid along seamlines of pieced striped fabric to embellish the new fabric.

How to Make Patchwork Fabrics

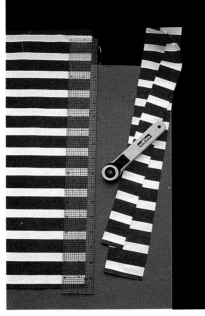

1) Cut crosswise strips from striped fabric the desired finished width plus ½" (1.3 cm) for seam allowances.

2) Realign strips, with color blocks staggered as desired. Pin, with right sides together and raw edges even; stitch ¼" (6 mm) seams. Finish edges, and press open.

Alternative. Cut soutache braid the length of seams. Center braid over seam, and apply (pages 102 and 103).

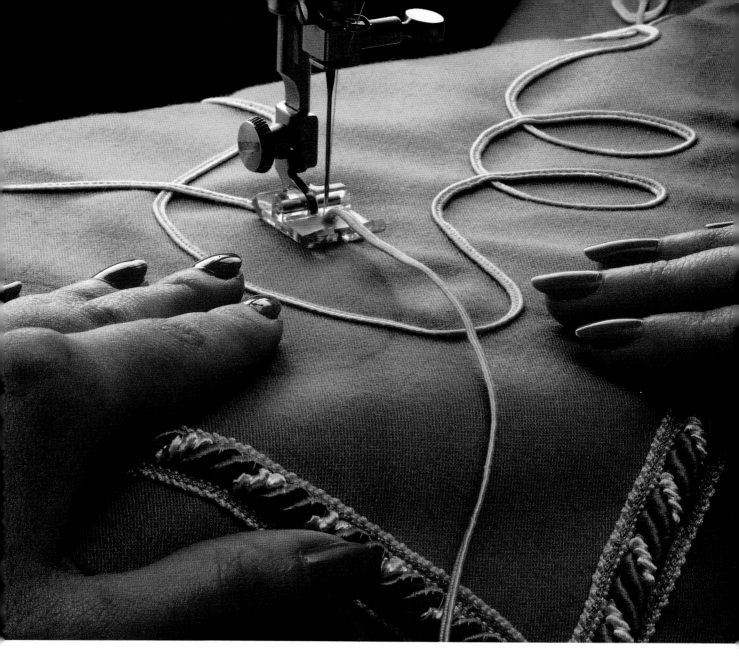

Machine-stitched Braids

Braid trim can create a look of elegance in a garment. The term, *passementerie*, refers to textured braids and to the use of braids in swirled designs on fabric. Passementerie can be used in many ways; to edge a jacket, to embellish the collar and cuffs of a blouse, or to accent the side seams of pants.

Preshrink braid before it is applied by steaming it with an iron held slightly above it. Or, if the braid is washable and being applied to a washable fabric, it can be soaked in hot tap water for ten minutes to preshrink it. Dry the braid on a towel; then press it with the right side down on the towel, to prevent flattening the texture of the braid.

Textured passementerie braids are traditionally hand-stitched in place, but they can be successfully machine-stitched for a faster method of application. If

the presser foot gets caught in the braid or does not ride evenly, remove the presser foot and machine-stitch without it, opposite.

For a neat finish, apply braids so they begin and end at a seam whenever possible. At corners, most flat braids can be folded into a miter. However, some braids, such as braids that have heavy cords, look best when they are eased around corners.

Soutache braid can be applied to fabric in decorative swirls, machine-stitching through the center of the soutache. It is not necessary to guide the soutache, if you thread it through plastic tape applied to the presser foot, as shown, opposite. This leaves your hands free to guide the fabric. If the fabric you are using is not stable, apply fusible interfacing to the wrong side.

Tips for Applying Passementerie Braid by Machine

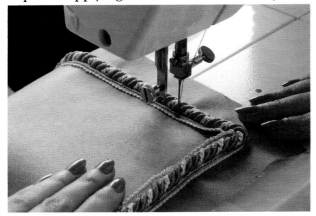

Baste braid in place, using liquid basting glue or glue stick. If braid has heavy cord, remove presser foot and lower presser foot lifter. Stitch, using matching or fine monofilament nylon thread and moving fabric along at a steady, even pace.

Begin and end braid at seam allowance when possible; stitch braid to each seam allowance ½" (1.3 cm) from edge. Ravel braid to stitching, and trim excess bulk. Stitch seam.

How to Apply Soutache Braid

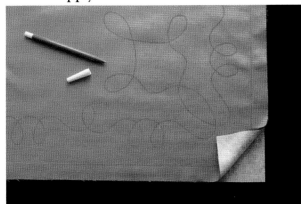

1) Mark design on fabric, using water-soluble marking pen or chalk. Place tear-away stabilizer under fabric in design area.

2) Place plastic tape on top of special-purpose presser foot; puncture tape at center of needle hole opening in presser foot, making hole the width of soutache braid.

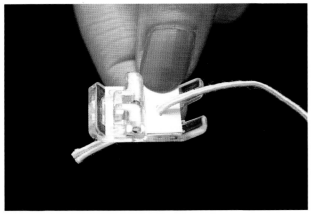

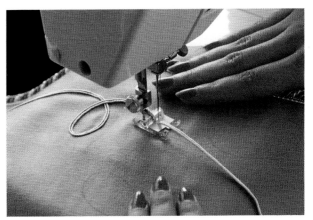

3) Place pressed soutache from front to back down through hole in tape. Replace presser foot on machine.

4) Stitch through center of soutache, using short stitch length, as you guide fabric so needle follows marked line; soutache feeds by itself. Remove stabilizer. Press lightly on wrong side of fabric.

Easy Edges

A pullover blouse can be edge-finished quickly by machine. A bias neckline facing with overlapped ends makes a neat neckline finish, and narrow machine-stitched hems finish the sleeves and lower edges of the blouse.

To make the bias facing, cut a 1¼" (3.2 cm) bias strip about 2" (5 cm) longer than the neck opening, to allow for overlap.

A narrow machine-stitched hem is nonbulky, making it suitable for lightweight or silky fabrics. It can also be used for hems on garments made from satin, taffeta, or organza. Horsehair braid can be added to this narrow hem for extra body.

Before stitching the hem, trim hem allowance to ⅜" (1 cm).

How to Sew a Narrow Hem

1) Machine-stitch ¼" (6 mm) from hem edge. Turn edge to wrong side on stitching line; press fold.

How to Sew a Bias Neckline Facing

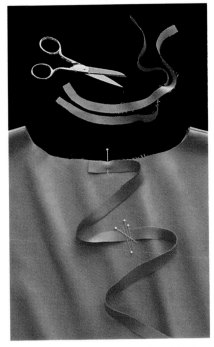

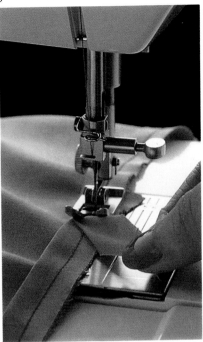

1) Cut bias facing, opposite. Fold strip in half lengthwise, *wrong* sides together; press. Trim garment seam allowance to ¼" (6 mm). Place strip on right side of garment, raw edges even, with end of strip 1" (2.5 cm) from center back.

2) Taper end of strip into seam allowance; stitch around neckline. Overlap ends, tapering other end into seam allowance.

3) Trim seam allowances. Press strip away from garment; then press it to inside of garment. Edgestitch around neckline from right side.

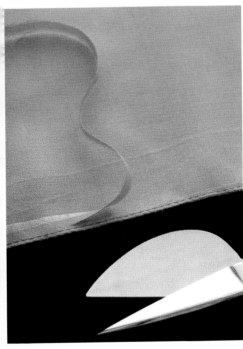

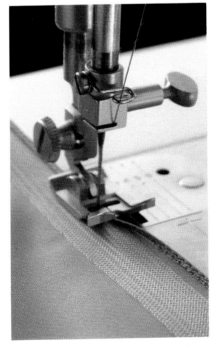

2) Stitch, using short stitch length, close to fold. Trim excess fabric close to stitching, using appliqué scissors. Press to remove fullness, if fabric has stretched.

3a) Turn hem edge to wrong side, enclosing raw edge. Stitch an even distance from edge.

3b) Turn hem edge to wrong side, enclosing raw edge. Slip horsehair braid into fold to add body to hem. Stitch an even distance from edge.

No-sag Coat Hem

When hemming a heavy fabric, as in a coat, it is helpful to distribute the weight by using multiple rows of stitches. A hem that is especially deep or heavy can have three or more rows of stitching to prevent the hem from sagging.

Interface the hem allowance, using hair canvas or fusible interfacing. Before stitching the hem, finish the raw edge with binding, overlocking, or zigzagging. Stitch the hem, using a loose catchstitch, so fabric does not pucker.

How to Hem Heavy Fabric

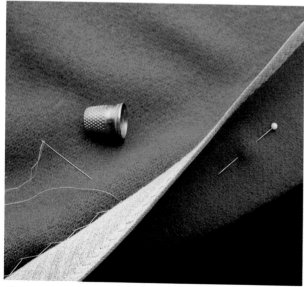

1) Interface hem allowance, and finish hem edge. Press hemline lightly; pin midway between hemline and hem edge. Fold back along pins, and catchstitch.

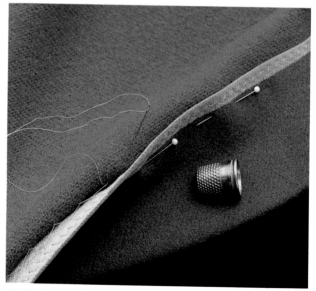

2) Pin hem edge in place, fold back edge along pins, and catchstitch loosely.

Invisible Hanging Hem

A hem looks best when it is virtually invisible, so it does not detract from the garment. A hanging hem suspended from organza not only prevents stitches from showing on the right side of a garment, but provides an underlining as well.

Adjust the skirt pattern for cutting the organza lining by subtracting twice the depth of the hem from the hem edge of the pattern and adding two seam allowance widths.

How to Sew a Hanging Hem

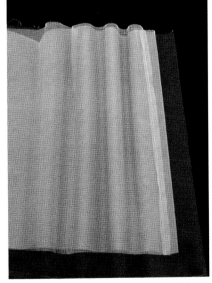

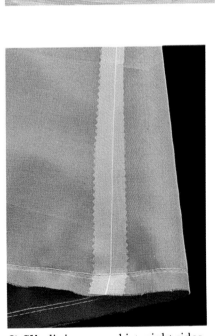

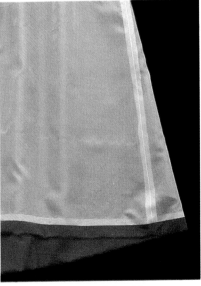

1) **Cut** organza lining, above. Stitch side seams in skirt and lining; press open. Easestitch hem edge of skirt.

2) **Slip** lining over skirt, right sides together. Pull up easestitching, so hem edges match. Machine-stitch edges together.

3) **Turn** garment right side out. Baste waistline edges together; press skirt lightly.

Just for Fun

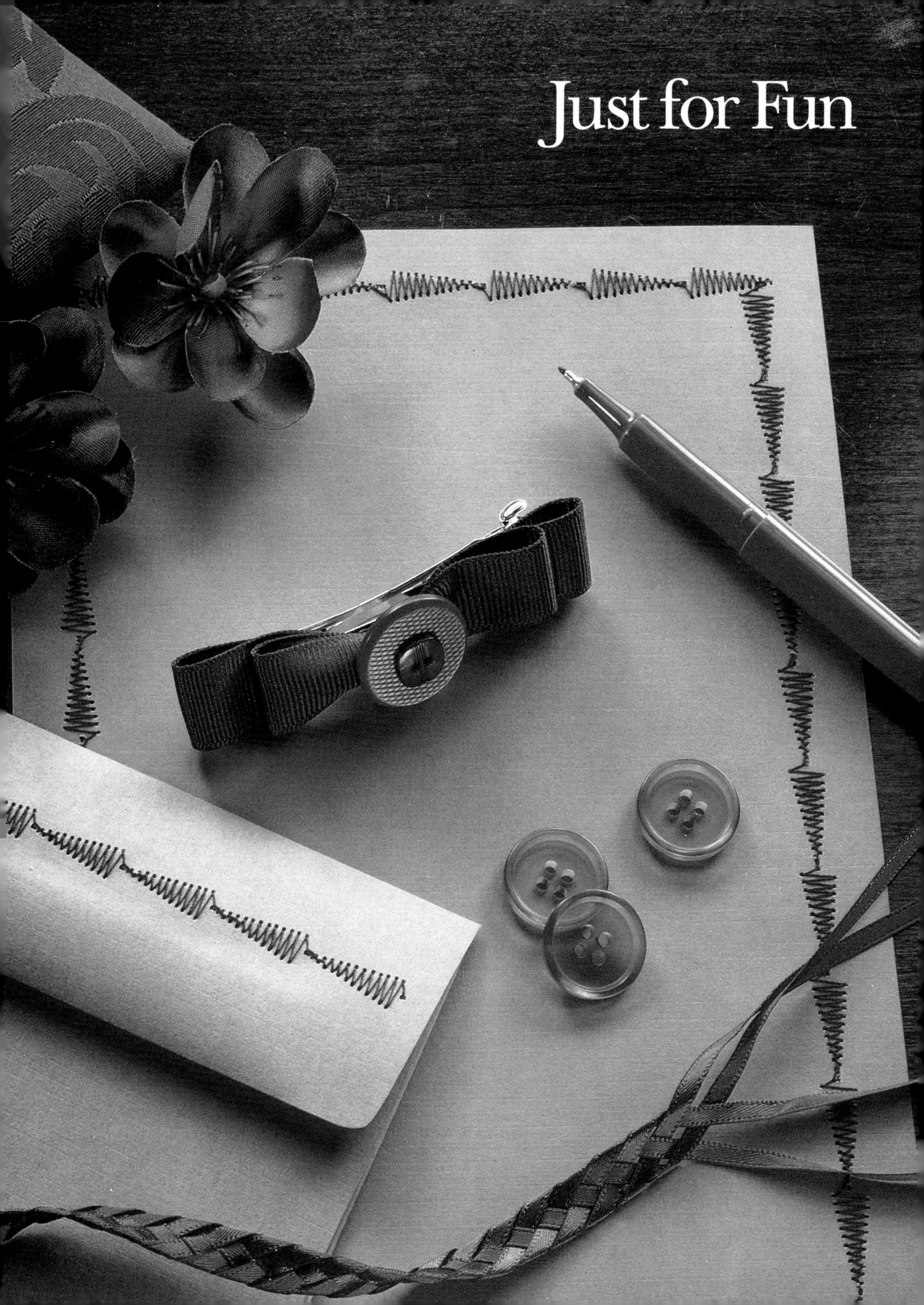

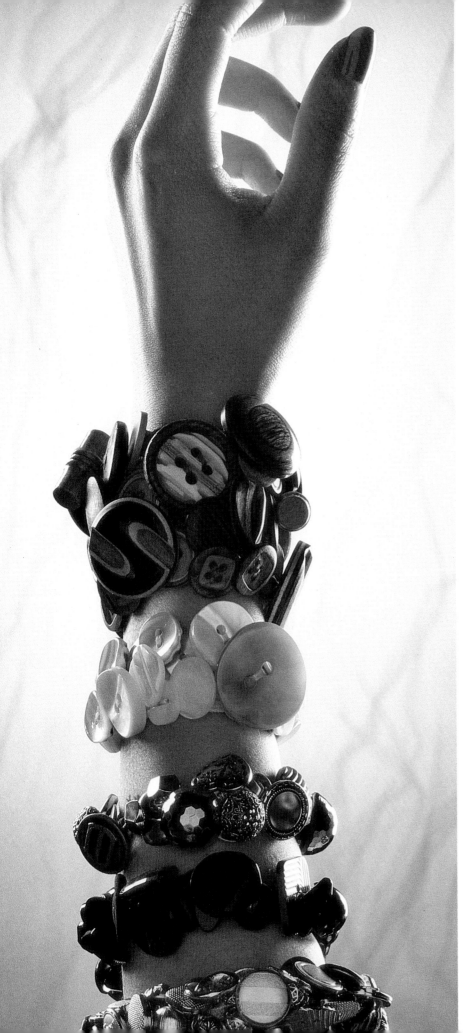

Fun Button Ideas

Sewers usually have a supply of buttons, because they save extra buttons from a project and salvage others from discarded garments. There are many creative ways of using these buttons.

To make button bracelets, choose elastic in the desired width and color. For a close fit, cut it the circumference of the arm plus allowance for overlap. Form the elastic into a loop, and stitch the ends together. Stitch buttons close together so they overlap, covering the elastic.

Cloth shoes and hair ornaments can be accented with buttons to coordinate with your outfit.

Earrings can be designed with a combination of buttons in various shapes and textures, using a color scheme to complement your clothing. Findings for making earrings are available at craft or jewelry supply stores.

Buttons & Bows

Buttons add a decorative touch, giving a basic garment a one-of-a-kind look.

Buttons and bows add interest to an otherwise plain garment. They can be functional or decorative.

Buttons can be stitched to the edge of a sleeve for an attractive cuff, below, or they can cover a design area such as the bow shape, left. Interface the design area to strengthen it for supporting the buttons. They can be sewn on quickly by machine before assembling a garment, or applied by hand to a ready-made garment. Use four strands of thread to secure buttons with just two stitches.

For centuries, bows have been used to decorate apparel. An easy method to tie a bow is shown, opposite. To keep the fabric or ribbon fresh, handle it as little as possible.

How to Tie Quick Bows

1) Form two equal loops, about 1" (2.5 cm) apart.

2) Cross one loop in front of other.

3) Wrap loop around back, and through center opening (arrow). Pull loops to adjust.

Chrysanthemums can be used to coordinate fabric shoes with a purse. For shoe ornaments, attach a large hook from a hook and eye set to the back of the chrysanthemum, and slide hook over edge of shoe. For purse ornaments, stitch the chrysanthemum directly to the purse flap.

Chrysanthemum Buttons

Chrysanthemum buttons are maneuvered through buttonholes by holding loops snugly together, then fluffing petals for a full, blooming appearance.

Fabric flowers add a finishing touch to an outfit when used as buttons or ornaments. Machine-made or bound buttonholes can be used with chrysanthemum buttons. Make test buttonholes in various sizes to find the size that works and looks best.

Use ¼" (6 mm) self-filled bias tubing to make these bowlike ornaments. To make the tubing, cut a bias strip of lightweight fabric 1 yard (.95 m) long and 1" (2.5 cm) wide for each chrysanthemum button. Fold the strip in half lengthwise, right sides together, and stitch a ¼" (6 mm) seam. Turn the tubing right side out, using a loop turner.

How to Make a Chrysanthemum Button

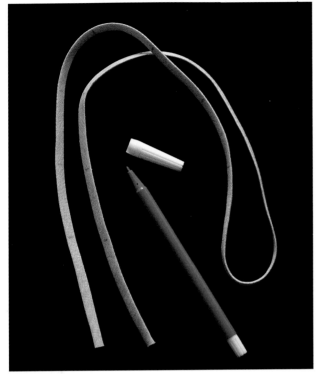

1) Mark 1 yd. (.95 m) of bias tubing every 2" (5 cm), beginning and ending 3" (7.5 cm) from each end of the tubing.

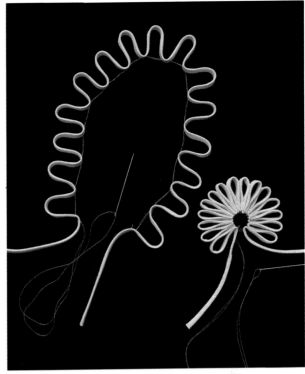

2) Stitch through each mark on tubing, using two strands of thread. Draw up tightly; arrange loops.

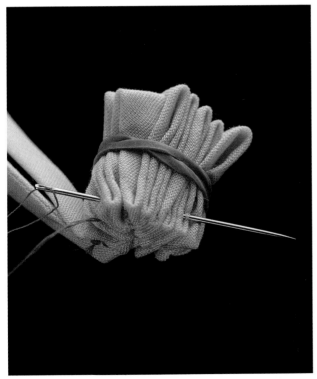

3) Gather all loops together, and secure with rubber band. Stitch loops in desired position, using two strands of thread.

4) Cut one end of tubing to within ⅜" (1 cm) of loops. Turn raw edge to inside; whipstitch to back of button. Cut other end to within 1" (2.5 cm) of loops. Turn raw edge to inside and whipstitch closed; make a shank by folding in half. Stitch securely to back of button.

Braided Ribbon Belt

A single ribbon can be a subtle statement of color on a garment; several ribbons, braided, can add yet another dimension.

Braided ribbons can be used as a belt. The width of the belt varies, depending on the width of the ribbon. A belt made from ⅝" (1.5 cm) ribbon will be about 1½" (3.8 cm) wide.

To make a braided ribbon belt, measure the waistline over the garment and add 1½" (3.8 cm) for finishing ends; ribbons will be braided to this length. Cut four lengths of double-faced ribbon, each length one-third longer than the desired length of braid. For example, if the braid will be 27" (68.5 cm), cut 36" (91.5 cm) of each ribbon.

Grosgrain ribbon is used for finishing the ends of the belt, because it is a durable ribbon. You will need a length of grosgrain ribbon ten times the width of the double-faced ribbon.

How to Make a Braided Ribbon Belt

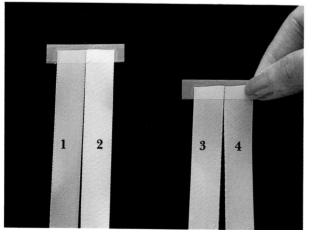

1) Join ribbons in two sets of two ribbons. Ribbons are now referred to as ribbon 1, ribbon 2, ribbon 3, and ribbon 4.

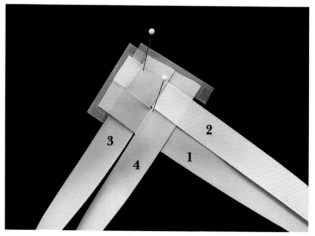

2) Pin ends of ribbons to a long, padded surface. Weave ribbon 2 under ribbon 3 and over ribbon 4. Weave ribbon 3 over ribbon 2 and under ribbon 1; weave ribbon 4 under ribbon 2 and over ribbon 1.

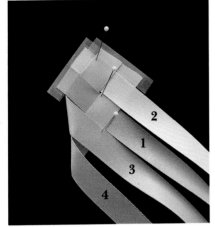

3) Fold ribbon 3 and ribbon 4 up and over to align them with ribbons 1 and 2.

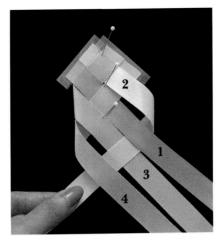

4) Fold ribbon 2 to the back; weave under ribbon 1, over ribbon 3, and under ribbon 4.

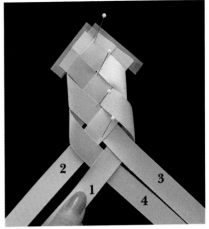

5) Fold ribbon 1 to the back, and weave under ribbon 3 and over ribbon 4.

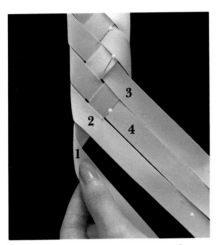

6) Fold ribbons 1 and 2 up and over to align them with ribbons 3 and 4.

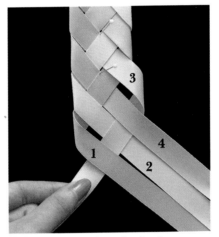

7) Fold ribbon 3 to the back; weave under ribbon 4, over ribbon 2, and under ribbon 1.

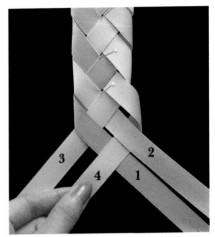

8) Fold ribbon 4 to the back; weave under ribbon 2 and over ribbon 1. Repeat steps 3 through 8 until braid is desired length.

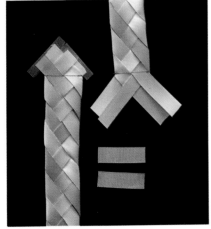

9) Stitch across ends at desired finished length of belt. Cut two strips of ⅝" (1.5 cm) grosgrain ribbon, each ½" (1.3 cm) longer than width of braid.

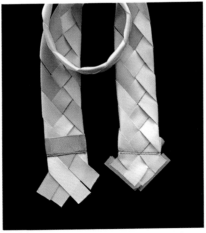

10) Turn under ends of grosgrain strips ¼" (6 mm). Place one long edge of strips on stitching lines, one on right side, one on wrong side. Stitch along edge of ribbon.

11) Trim braid seam allowance to ¼" (6 mm). Fold back strips, enclosing ends of braid; handstitch into place. Apply fasteners.

Silk Flower Appliqués

Silk flowers can be used to make attractive appliqués. They can embellish garments, including evening gowns and casual wear, or they can be used to make a shadow box picture.

If you intend to wash the project, test the flowers for colorfastness by dipping them in soapy water and rinsing them. This is especially important for red or dark colors.

To appliqué silk flowers on a garment, take the flowers apart and remove any wires or florist tape. Then shape the petals into new flowers, and stitch them to the garment (pages 119 to 121). Petals from two flowers can be combined into one to vary the look.

When using silk flowers in a shadow box, it is not necessary to remove all the wires from the petals and stems; they may be helpful in shaping the flowers. The flowers may be glued, instead of stitched, into the shadow box.

Plan the placement of the flowers on your project before you begin, marking the placement line for the stem and the general spacing of the main flowers.

Use lightweight monofilament nylon thread to apply silk flowers; it is invisible and does not detract from the flowers. All-purpose thread may be used to stitch the stems. (Contrasting thread is used to show detail in the photos that follow.)

Tips for Appliquéing Silk Flowers

Layer two or more single-layer flowers. Stitch to project through center of flower. Hand-stitch pearl, seed pearls, or button to flower.

Pinch two or more layers of petals at center, and gather by hand to create a full blossom; stitch through layers at base of flower. Stitch in place on project.

Place tear-away stabilizer under fabric in stem area. Zigzag over yarn to make stem; remove stabilizer. Attach leaves to project by stitching along center vein.

How to Shape Petals to Form a Flower

1) Strip petals from stem; remove wires and stamens.

2) Roll petal into bud shape and stitch through layers; use as a bud or as center petal of a flower. To start shaping flower, wrap another petal around center petal, ¼" (6 mm) higher than center petal.

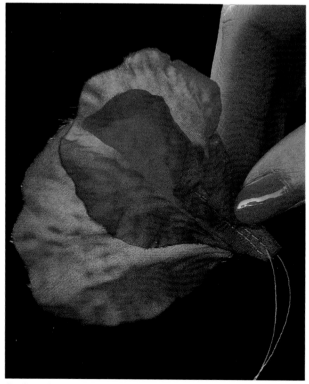

3) Continue wrapping desired number of petals around center petal.

4) Stitch back and forth through base of flower, by machine or by hand, to secure petals.

5) Fold petals back to achieve desired shape. Tack one petal to another, as necessary, to shape flower; work from center of flower outward.

6) Trim off base of flower next to stitching. Stitch trimmed base to garment at desired location, stitching over previous stitches.

7) Fold back one or two outer petals at the top of flower, and stitch them to garment to prevent flower from drooping.

8) Fold back one or two outer petals at the bottom of flower, and stitch them to garment, covering trimmed base of flower.

Secrets of Lace Embroidery

Make a garment special by adding an inset yoke of delicate lace embroidery. Or create a lace collar that can be used with many different garments.

Lace can be embroidered on a conventional sewing machine, with the presser foot removed; on some machines, a darning foot may be used. Two layers of

tulle are placed over water-soluble stabilizer and held firmly in an embroidery hoop.

The lace is stitched with a fine needle and machine embroidery thread. Or use silk or rayon thread to add luster to the embroidery stitches. Stitch over the design several times for more definition.

How to Make Embroidered Lace

1) Transfer embroidery design to the tulle, using a water-soluble marking pen.

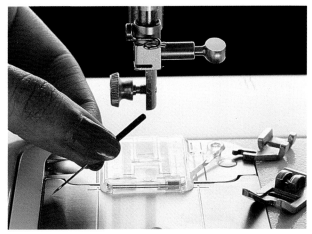

2) Remove presser foot. Cover feed dogs with feed cover plate, or lower them. Loosen tension, and release pressure on presser foot. Insert fine needle.

3) Place two layers of tulle, with a double layer of water-soluble stabilizer underneath, upside down in embroidery hoop. Place hoop under needle. Lower presser foot lifter to control tension on upper thread.

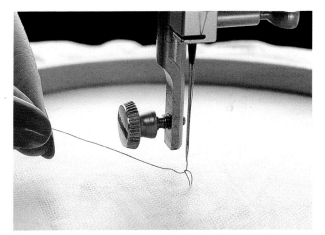

4) Set machine for straight stitching. Rotate the handwheel, while holding needle thread, to bring bobbin thread to the top of the work. Stitch several stitches in one spot to anchor threads. Clip thread tails.

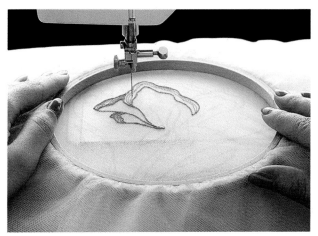

5) Hold hoop flat against bed of the machine with both hands. Run the machine at a steady pace, and trace the outline of design, using the needle as a pencil; keep hoop facing in one direction.

6) Remove lace and stabilizer from hoop. Carefully tear away as much of the stabilizer as possible. Dip lace in cold water to remove any traces of stabilizer and marking pen. Press.

Perforating Paper

The decorative stitches on the sewing machine can be used to create unusual greeting cards or stationery. Use firm paper, a large needle, and a long stitch length.

Practice stitching designs on typing paper with and without thread in the machine. Some designs may be lost without the use of thread to connect the holes; others may be too complex and simply destroy the paper. When using thread, use any machine embroidery thread, or experiment with different kinds of threads, such as metallics. When thread is not used, it is possible to stack and perforate paper in layers.

Test designs, using different needles. A wing needle makes a slit in the paper; twin needles duplicate designs side by side.

Ways to Use Perforated Paper

Business cards can be decorated with a stitched border to add a creative touch.

Stationery sheets and the flaps of envelopes can be perforated or stitched with thread.

Place cards can be embellished by stitching over decorative ribbon for a festive touch.

Index

Cy DeCosse Incorporated offers
sewing accessories to subscribers.
For information write:

Sewing Accessories
5900 Green Oak Drive
Minnetonka, MN 55343